Rent-Seeking and
Economic Growth in Africa

Rent-Seeking and Economic Growth in Africa

Mark Gallagher

Westview Press

BOULDER • SAN FRANCISCO • OXFORD

HB
401
G35
1991

This Westview softcover edition is printed on acid-free paper and bound in library-quality, coated covers that carry the highest rating of the National Association of State Textbook Administrators, in consultation with the Association of American Publishers and the Book Manufacturers' Institute.

Copyright © 1991 by Westview Press, Inc.

Published in 1991 in the United States of America by Westview Press, Inc., 5500 Central Avenue, Boulder, Colorado 80301, and in the United Kingdom by Westview Press, 36 Lonsdale Road, Summertown, Oxford OX2 7EW

A CIP catalog record for this book is available from the Library of Congress.
ISBN 0-8133-8283-1

Printed and bound in the United States of America

The paper used in this publication meets the requirements of the American National Standard for Permanence of Paper for Printed Library Materials Z39.48-1984.

10   9   8   7   6   5   4   3   2   1

Contents

Tables and Figures

Tables

Figures

Preface

My interest in Africa's development began when the U.S. Agency for International Development first sent me to Liberia as a foreign service officer in 1984. Several years in the field showed me that understanding Africa's economic difficulties required a better understanding of the forces that cause inefficiency and hamper growth. The usual economic variables, such as investment, labor growth, changes in international terms of trade, and foreign aid, do not explain the differences in growth among African countries nor the declines in per capita incomes. Indeed, neo-classical growth theories cannot explain declining per capita incomes. Also, neo-classical growth theories, without great elaboration and numerous "shift variables," lead one to expect greater economic growth in Africa than elsewhere. The exact opposite has been true.

Numerous studies have suggested that policy reforms would improve Africa's growth. One wonders why after so many years of failed policies African countries find it so difficult to reform. Clearly, someone benefits from bad policies.

The notion that someone is benefitting from bad policies naturally raises the concept of rent-seeking. The problem, however, is that until recently most theorists (including Gordon Tullock, one of the granddaddies of rent-seeking theory) have held that rent-seeking creates inefficiency and is welfare reducing, but that it should not slow growth. This seemed a big problem.

This book derives a formal, general model where individuals seek to maximize their income from a combination of productive and rent-seeking activities. Rents are aggregated for 22 African countries, based on methods developed in this book, for the periods

1975-1981 and 1981-87. Political pluralism is a proxy for institutional competition for rents. The greater the institutional competition for rents the less attractive rent-seeking is vis-a-vis productive use of resources. The model is then put into a dynamic framework and is compared to the neo-classical growth model using ordinary and non-linear least squares regressions. The rent-seeking model generally outperforms the neo-classical growth model in explaining resource use and economic growth in Africa. The nature of the rent-seeking society is also investigated.

Government's role in the growth process in Africa is also examined. Government has been a major source of investment and human capital spending, contributing to growth. On the other hand, government resource allocation is usually inefficient and leads to rent-seeking. Overall, the size of the government sector is inversely related to growth.

Shocks, such as coups d' etat, civil strife, war, drought, floods, etc. have been detrimental to investment and economic growth but explain only part of Africa's poor growth performance. Although treated as exogenous, man-made shocks could probably be attributed to poor economic performance, prevalence of rent-seeking, and other factors.

I wish to thank Joe Reid, who over numerous telephone calls and occasional beer and pizza kept me on track, challenging me to increase rigor and sharpen the presentation. The World Bank provided me with the use of its library and other facilities, data, and access to intellectually stimulating colleagues. Without such an advantage this project could not have been possible. In addition, I benefitted greatly from comments and questions I received on the basic model that I presented in an African Technical Department, Trade and Finance Division seminar held at the World Bank in October 1990.

Of course, all remaining errors and misunderstandings are my own fault. The opinions and classifications used in this book do not necessarily reflect the views of the World Bank.

My wife, Cathy, who deserves a medal of honor for putting up with me while I prepared this manuscript, has been my greatest resource and comfort. Melissa -- my sometimes research assistant -- and Megan and Cara are the most wonderful daughters in the world and have cheered me up and kept me going when the going got rough. My parents and my in-laws have given moral support and much encouragement. In addition, thanks go to Spencer Carr, Amy Eisenberg, and Lynn Arts, all of Westview Press, each of whom has given me encouragement in completing this project as well as valuable guidance and editorial assistance.

Mark Gallagher
Africa Technical Department
World Bank

1

Introduction

This chapter reviews the recent economic performance of Sub-Saharan Africa,[1] discusses the development paradigms prevailing at African independence, provides a rationale for studying economic growth in an African setting, and outlines the rest of this book.

Economic Perfomance in Africa

Africa's economic performance since independence has been dismal and has been getting worse. Between 1965 and 1973 average population weighted GDP growth in Africa was 5.9 percent per annum (p.a.), about two points above population growth.[2] From 1973 to 1980 this growth slowed to only 2.5 percent p.a., about a point below population growth. And, by the 1980s (1980-87) GDP growth was crawling along at only 0.5 percent p.a., about three points below population growth. These data imply that living standards have been on the decline in most of Africa since the mid-1970s.

These average values mask a great diversity of experiences. For instance, per capita GDP in Chad declined by about 3 percent p.a. in the 1970s and in Zaire by almost 4 percent p.a. in the same period. By the end of the 1980s per capita income in Liberia was only half what it had been at the end of the 1970s. This is contrasted by the stellar performances of Botswana, where per capita GDP has more than doubled from the mid-1970s to the mid-1980s, Mauritius, where GDP has been growing by about 5.5 percent p.a. for the past fifteen years, and Cape Verde, Senegal, Swaziland, and Kenya, where economic growth has generally outpaced population growth.[3]

Economic growth has been slower in the 1980s compared to either the 1970s or the 1960s. So, too, has gross domestic investment, which during 1973-80 grew by about 4 percent p.a. in real terms but in the 1980s averaged about an 8 percent decline. A great deal of the decline can be attributed to a drying up in international liquidity triggered by Mexico's de facto international debt default in 1982. A few countries, however, have managed to retain some growth in investment. For instance, Mauritius, with its liberal trade and investment policies, has enjoyed investment growth of over 10 percent p.a. in the 1980s. Ghana, after investment declined by almost 4 percent p.a. in the 1970s, has seen some recovery and investment has been growing at over 3 percent p.a. in the 1980s, although it will be a long time before the capital stock is restored to 1970 levels.

The general African experience, to repeat, is economic decline. Africa's dismal economic performance is showing up in terms of social indicators. For instance, food availability, as measured by average daily caloric intake, grew by only .5 percent p.a. in Africa during the 1980s, while growing by 1.7 percent p.a. in Latin America and the Caribbean, by 5.7 percent p.a. in the Middle East and North Africa, and 4.9 percent p.a. in Asia and the Pacific. The availability of pharmaceuticals in Africa[4] has been declining at least since 1980, while continuing to rise in Asia and the Pacific and possibly declining more slowly in the Middle East and Latin America. Gross primary school enrollment ratios were no higher in the mid-1980s, on average, than at the beginning of the decade, and in a number of countries enrollment ratios have declined. Per capita education and health spending in African countries are no greater today than ten years ago. Indeed, social spending per capita is lower than it had been for almost half of the countries for which data are available.

In sum, although the experiences of African countries are mixed, with a few having done quite well, some managing to get by, and the majority experiencing rapid pauperization, overall economic performance has been poor and the effects are being felt in the social sectors and the quality of life.

Structure of African Economies

African economies differ from other economies in significant ways. The share of manufacturing in Africa's low income economies[5] only averages about 8 percent of GDP compared to 24 percent for all low income countries.[6] The differences in manufacturing for middle income Africa persist, amounting to only 11 percent (1980) versus 22 percent for all middle income countries. Also, African countries tend to be somewhat more services oriented (about 42 percent versus 32 percent).

Compared to other low income countries, African economies have large public sectors. For instance, central government spending in GDP was over 25 percent for African countries during the 1980s, while it was not even 20 percent in Asian low income countries.[7] In Latin America the share was about the same as in Africa. Regulation of investment, allocation of investible funds, controls on foreign exchange and high implicit taxes on agriculture have been rampant in Africa.

The next section provides an inventory of policy reforms being espoused by African leaders.

Policy Reforms in Africa

This section presents the range of policy reforms that policy makers in Africa announced between 1984-87.[8] The purpose is not to assess the need for these reforms nor to evaluate how or whether these reforms have actually been implemented. While it is conceded that planned reforms may diverge greatly from implementation, this inventory of policy reform intentions is necessary to get a clear picture of the range and depth of reform needed in Africa.[9]

Of the forty countries surveyed, fully twenty-nine had fiscal reform programs. These were mainly to reduce deficit spending. Although most included greater tax effort and reduced expenditures, six of the twenty-nine countries did not specifically include greater tax effort. Twelve countries have announced major tax reforms.

Reduction in wages and salaries and other civil service reforms were on the reform agenda of twenty-four countries, but increased wages and salaries (rates) were planned for Ghana and Uganda, where government wages had fallen behind those in the rest of the country. A tightening of money growth was planned in twelve countries. Tight money policies were generally advocated in countries attempting to reduce their fiscal deficits. Studies of the money and banking systems, prior to announcing reforms, were called for in four countries.

Although only eight countries had devalued their currencies per se, another twelve have or intend to liberalize their foreign exchange markets, some by means of foreign exchange auctions. Liberalization of the trade regimes, which includes removal of quantitative restrictions, tariff reform, elimination of import/export monopolies, among other things, have been included in policy reform agenda in sixteen countries.

Studies of the public enterprise sector have been planned in six countries. In most cases public enterprise reform has concentrated on management improvements, as well as institutional and budgetary reforms. But privatization has taken place or planned, to a limited degree, in fourteen of the twenty-eight countries where public enterprise reform is on the policy reform agenda.

Agricultural reforms are planned or have been implemented in twenty countries, and studies with reform in mind have been promised in another two. In thirteen of these countries increased producer prices have been called for, reduction in input subsidies in six, and improved market access -- including decontrol, elimination of monopoly/monopsony, and certain investment -- in ten.

Decontrol of general prices has taken place or has been planned for eleven countries, elimination or reduction of consumer subsidies for five, increases in electricity tariffs for six, and price increases for petroleum products for eight.

The general thrust of these reforms is the reduction of the state's role in African economies; through reduced regulation and smaller government, in general.[10]

Development Paradigms at Independence

Upon gaining independence many African governments opted for a development path that included considerable governmental intervention in allocating economic resources. Policies, while often stated in terms of African Socialism, were not out of line with the received economic development theories of the time. Allocation of investment to public enterprises, non-market allocation of foreign exchange, controlled prices and restrictions on both domestic and foreign capital were not only consistent with African Socialism but also with the major streams of thought among development theorists of the period. African leaders, and development theorists, believed that development investment must lead to balanced growth, make up for lack of domestic entrepreneurs, and provide stimulus and protection to domestic industry. Furthermore, African leaders were often suspicious of international capital and trade. The need to industrialize was seen as urgent. Such industrialization was to come about through government direct investment in the productive processes and through government planning and control.

The origin of this prevalent development paradigm in this century can be traced to G.S. Fel'man, who provided a theoretical base for the Soviet Union's equating modernization with industrialization. Capital and labor were seen as more productive in industry compared to agriculture. Industry provided economies of scale and external economies while agriculture was subject to diminishing returns.[11] Later work by Mahalonobis, as well as by Fel'man, was related to the Harrod-Domar model of economic growth. Increase in the capital stock was the source of growth, and it was to industry that increased capital stock was to be allocated for the further production of capital rather than consumer goods. Agriculture had to provide the savings necessary for investment in manufacturing and to spur the trade and service sectors.

Free trade was seen as anathema to the development process. According to Prebisch (1950), if LDCs concentrated on the export of those goods where they had a natural comparative advantage they would be relegated to the production and export of primaries and the importation of manufactures. Because of the respective income and price elasticities the poor countries would face continuing deterioration in their terms of trade and would not be able to achieve the objectives of development. Gunnar Myrdal (1957) was also in favor of protecting domestic manufactures production since he felt that international trade does not work toward equality in the remuneration to factors of production. If left to its own course economic development under free trade tends to award favors to those who are already well endowed and even to thwart the efforts of those who happen to live in regions that are lagging behind.

Of course these trade pessimists were not unchallenged. For instance, J.R. Hicks (1959) pointed out the near impossibility of developing countries, especially small ones, of producing the adequate capital goods, at reasonable cost, that would be needed for the development process. Kravis (1970) argued that the trade pessimists incorrectly concentrated on the demand side and pointed out that the export expansion of the US, Canada and Australia in the last century came about not through demand changes but through supply changes. In short, Kravis says that the progress of those countries came about not from favorable external demand but from successful economic development. Despite a few voices of dissent however, the import substitution apostles had taken the lead in the power of ideas.

Central planning was at its high point in the development literature. Economic planning for the developing countries immediately following the second world war embraced the concept of import substitution, a perceived need for rapid industrialization, a 1930s distaste for capitalism, and the rise of demand management of the Keynesian school. According to Stanislaw Welisz (1971), "when development planning was in its infancy, well-known economists[12] ranging in opinion from the liberal right to the Marxian left advocated planning as the fastest and least painful path to growth." In 1946 Rosenstein-Rodan argued that there were many reasons to show why "the whole of industry was to be treated and planned like one huge firm or trust." According to Mandelbaum in 1947:

> the theory of state financed expansion of demand is by now so undisputed, and there are so many historical precedents to confirm it, that more need not be said. We assume that this method will be chosen whenever the need for

industrialization is so strongly felt that slow changes and exclusive reliance upon private initiative no longer suffice. . . . Even apart from the USSR there are many instances in recent history of industrialization where the assumption by the state of entrepreneurial functions has accelerated the modernization of equipment and reduced the disadvantages which formerly characterized the position of backward countries.

Other prominent economists of the time were also in favor of state intervention and state-centric development strategies. To name just a few: Walt Rostow, Hollis Chenery and Hans Singer. The usual reasons had to do with market failure -- such as, "myopia of the general public," forward and backward linkages which created technical externalities and were sometimes the rationale for "balanced growth" and other times for "unbalanced growth," inadequate social overhead capital, etc. -- which was seen as particularly prevalent in developing countries.

In sum, for the first two decades of the post-World War II era economic development theorists generally recommended a state directed, internally oriented, industry-biased path to rapid economic development. In recent years there has been a return to more classical economic beliefs -- that the market is the better allocater of a nation's resources, that free international trade enhances both welfare and growth, and that market failure may not always imply the need for government intervention. African countries became independent when these state-centric theories were dominant. With the change in direction and the reversion to more classical approaches to economic development many African governments have been claiming to restructure their economies -- to liberalize trade, deregulate markets and investment and reduce the scope of government in these economies. In the next section I discuss why Africa is the focus of this study.

Why Africa?

There are several reasons for focusing this study on Africa. For one, although there is great diversity among African countries there are sufficient cultural, historical, and political commonalities to allow for application of <u>cet. par.</u> techniques. In general there are more distortions and general non-market decision-making in Africa than in other parts of the world. Africa made a lot of poor decisions, in part because of inappropriate advice from development theorists in industrialized countries. After twenty or thirty years of dismal performance some assessment on a pan-African basis is warranted.

Africa has been suffering from slow, no or negative growth since independence. Neo-classical growth theory does not allow for economic decline. Indeed, according to the basic neo-classical growth model we should have expected growth in Africa to have outpaced growth in the rest of the world. This makes Africa a suitable region for exploring alternative theories of growth, political economy and resource allocation.

At the same time, Africa has become the focus of policy reformers. Structural Adjustment Programs of the World Bank, Stabilization Programs of the International Monetary Fund, and the myriad of policy reforms that African leaders have pledged to implement have not yet brought Africa to a state of recovery, let alone, rapid economic growth. Even if such reforms can be shown to improve efficiency and generate new economic growth, it remains uncertain if such growth will be sustainable. Will the new growth path require a degree of confidence in the stability of African economies, regimes and property rights?

Additionally, a number of empirical studies of growth have included African countries,[13] where African economies are indicated with a dummy variable. African countries have experienced slower growth, which is distinctly indicated in these empirical tests, leading us to conclude that something is happening in Africa that is not going on in other regions of the world, and is unexplained by these cross-country studies.

Outline of This Book

In Chapter 2 economic growth models, the rent-seeking literature and theories of the state are surveyed. It is proposed that these three bodies of literature might be melded to yield a better understanding of the growth process. Chapter 3 presents an extended theory of competitive rent-seeking and yields a number of hypotheses about economic growth, policies and institutions of the state, especially as applied to Africa.

Chapter 4 presents a general economic growth model based on the theory of Chapter 3. The model includes two sectors, one productive the other destroying resources in rent-seeking. The model tests for competitive rent-seeking, the implications of institutional competition for rents and impact on economic growth. Chapter 4 also investigates the incidence of rents, i.e., where rent-seeking is greatest.

Chapter 5 presents the major conclusions. This chapter also indicates a number of studies that might be undertaken to better understand rent-seeking and its relationship to growth and how countries are governed.

An appendix provides detailed notes on data quality, sources, and methodology as well as providing the data used in the estimations of Chapter 4. A second appendix summarizes notes on African regimes.

Notes

1. Hereafter referred to as Africa.

2. Data are from Table 2 in Sub-Saharan Africa: From Crisis to Sustainable Growth, World Bank (1989).

3. Data in this paragraph can be found in various tables in Gallagher (1989) and Gallagher and Ogbu (1989).

4. Measured by nominal value in US dollars of pharmaceutical imports.

5. By international convention, low income countries are those eligible for IDA (International Development Agency) borrowing. For the most part, a county's eligibility is determined by its per capita income, as measured according to the "Atlas Method." The cut-off per capita income level changes annually. In 1989, 32 African countries were classified as "low income."

6. Data are for 1987 and are taken from World Bank (1989) and (1988).

7. Central government spending in Western Europe is about the same on average as in Africa, while in the US central government spending is only about 20% of GDP.

8. The period was chosen because of the availability of documentation and because it coincided with the period when many of Africa's reform programs began.

9. I collected the information from various IMF and World Bank documents, including: Article IV Consultations, Recent Economic Developments, Country Economic Memoranda, Invitations to Negotiate Structural Adjustment Credits, Policy Framework Papers, as well as some documents issued by African governments. Only those policy reforms that were

actually agreed to by African governments were included in the survey. Policy recommendations made in Bank and Fund documents that were not explicitly agreed to by the respective government -- such agreement can be made by closing on a standby, CFF, SAL or other such agreement -- are excluded.

10. For an evaluation of reform implementation, see Gallagher (1990-91).

11. Indeed, diminishing returns to agriculture can also be traced back to Malthus and Ricardo.

12. Welisz does not mention who these well-know economists, left or right, are.

13. See Grier and Tullock (1989), Barro (1989a&b), and Easterly and Wetzel (1989).

2

Growth, Rent-Seeking, and the State

This chapter surveys the literature on economic growth models, rent-seeking and the role of the state in the development process.

There are a number of purposes to this survey. This survey presents the development of mainstream growth theories in a chronological and logical order but with special emphasis on the formal models as have been developed since Keynes and with some discussion of some empirical relationships that have been found between policy variables and economic growth. The survey of the rent-seeking literature is similar, but also clarifies terminology for this relatively new field of economics. The surveys of growth and rent-seeking demand some concept of the role of the state. Theories of the state predate Aristotle. Rather than surveying the entire field I discuss some of the more current debates on the role of the state in growth and rent-seeking.

Growth Models

There have been many attempts to find the sources of economic growth. Some relate social phenomena to growth such as in Scholing and Timmermann (1988). Others relate economic growth to specific economic variables. For instance, Gemmel (1983), Landau (1983 and 1986), and Grossmann (1988) all relate economic growth to the size of Government -- all finding a negative relationship. Others, such as

Chenery and Taylor (1968), Chenery and Syrquin (1975), Wood (1986), and Lewis (1978) relate the structure of production -- the roles of industry, trade and agriculture -- to economic growth. In sum, the growth literature represents a potpourri of perspectives on the sources of economic growth. In the following pages I review a mass of literature, but restrict myself to the following broad topics: Keynesian and neo-classical models, human capital, recent developments in growth models, and some empirical results of policy-determined growth models.

Keynesian Models. Keynesian models are characterized by their concentration on savings and investment with no regard to optimizing behavior of economic agents. The Keynesian models generally assume that government policies that affect national savings and investment can accelerate growth. Indeed, these models imply the necessity of government intervention.

In the Harrod-Domar model output is a function of capital stock and economic growth is a function of investment. The model:

$Q = vK$, that is, Q, output is a multiple of the level of capital.

This can be manipulated to yield the capital output ratio:

$Q/K = v$ and

$1/v = K/Q =$ the capital output ratio.

From the first equation the change in output is equal to the inverse of the capital-output ratio multiplied by the change in the capital stock: $\Delta Q = v\Delta K$. The Harrod-Domar model is both simple and manageable. It is simple in that it indicates a direct linear relationship between investment and economic growth. It is manageable since, although data on capital stock are not easily aggregated, aggregate investment expenditures are generally reported as part of the national accounts.

Perhaps the simplicity and manageability of the Harrod-Domar model provided some impetus for its wide reception among development economists. Indeed, after so many subsequent improvements on economic growth models the incremental-capital-output ratio is still reported as a basic economic indicator for developing countries.[1] At any rate, a very great deal of emphasis has been placed on the rate of investment, or capital accumulation, as the means of achieving growth.

The Lewis (1954) model also relies on investment in the modern sector as the sole source of growth. Lewis saw labor in the "traditional" sector as being in surplus and its marginal product being less than its average product (this implies some labor was subsidizing other labor). Expansion could only occur through investment in the "modern" sector as surplus laborers would be transferred from essentially non-productive work in the traditional sector to the modern sector with little or no cost in terms of traditional sector output.

Lewis (1954) relied upon the classical notion that savings are only from profits, but the model is Keynesian in that it assumes slack resources (labor) and that growth comes entirely from investment. Also, Lewis suggests that inflationary policies will generate an expansion of credit[2] which will increase modern sector investment. The increase in modern sector investment will raise industrial output and hence drive prices back down to their original levels. In this way expansionary policies are not inflationary.

Rostow (1960) offers an alternative to the Keynesian models, but retains several important elements, namely the predominance of the role of capital and a rationale for government intervention. He saw growth, or development, as progression through a series of stages ("stages of growth"). Once certain social preconditions are attained a society could only advance into the "take-off" stage of development when a threshold of capital accumulation is reached. Capital accumulation could be encouraged (managed) through fiscal policies or through foreign borrowing.

The Keynesian models have three key factors in common. They attribute all growth to investment, with labor assumed to be in ample or surplus supply. Even Rostow, once preconditions had been met, saw saving cum investment as the key to the take-off stage. No sort of optimizing behavior relates savings to investment nor investment to the return on investment. In the Lewis model workers in the traditional sector are assumed to behave in a non-economic manner, where some workers subsidize the consumption of others and no one is paid according to his or her marginal contribution to output. Finally, the Keynesian models are mechanistic, relying on adding a

single homogenous ingredient (investment) to gain economic growth.
If this magic ingredient is not already available it can easily be
generated by expansionary fiscal and monetary policies.

Neo-Classical Models.[3] Solow pointed out the basic instability of
the Harrod-Domar model, which he described as a "knife-edge" of
economic growth. Solow's criticism basically can be explained in the
following description of the Harrod-Domar model.

Output (Q) is produced with a Leontief technology, where it is a
function of fixed proportions of capital (K) and labor (L). For
example,

$$Q = \min[\frac{K}{\alpha}, \frac{L}{\beta}]$$

In this model if capital grows more rapidly than labor then capital
will be in excess supply. If capital does not grow as rapidly as the
labor supply then there will be growing unemployment. Indeed, if the
economy begins from a position of unemployment then even if capital
and labor grow at the same rate[4] unemployment will persist, although
it will diminish asymptotically. The model is inherently unstable. If
the model should start out in equilibrium, i.e., without excess capital
or labor, there is no equilibrating mechanism to restore equilibrium
after a shock to the system.

Although Solow showed how more realistic assumptions would
yield a stable model of economic growth, I will just discuss the
simplest example, where he uses the Cobb-Douglas production
function. The basic point is, if the fixed coefficients production
function is replaced by a production function where capital and labor
are substitutes for each other and where each exhibits diminishing
returns, then the system will tend toward stable economic growth. For
example,

$$Q = K^{\alpha}L^{1-\alpha}$$

and L grows at the rate of n,then capital is accumulated as investment
equal to the amount of saving,

$$\frac{dK}{dt} = sK^{\alpha}[L_0 e^{nt}]^{1-\alpha}$$

which can be directly integrated,

$$K(t) = [K_0^b - \frac{s}{n}L_0 e^{nbt}]$$

where $b=1-\alpha$, K_0 is the initial capital stock.

As t increases (i.e., as time goes by) K(t) grows essentially at the same rate as the labor force and the capital-labor ratio remains constant. Additionally, asymptotically, Q must grow at the same rate as K and L, that is at the relative rate n. Real income per head of the labor force, Q/L tends to the value $(s/n)^{\alpha/b}$. With the Cobb-Douglas production function it is always true that $Q/L = (K/L)^{\alpha}$ and therefore the equilibrium level of K/Q is s/n. Keeping in mind that K/Q is the same as the capital output ratio of the Harrod-Domar model then K/Q = s/n, therefore n = s/(K/Q), which means that the "natural" rate equals the "warranted" rate, not as a matter of happenstance, or government policy, but as the result of market forces.

Solow proceeds to show how unemployment arising from a fixed wage could persist in the neo-classical model as well as how monetary imbalances could lead to idle capital, but these are not the major contributions to the field.

In the steady state output, saving, investment, population and consumption all grow at the same rate. Once in the steady state there is no way for living standards to improve as a result of increased investment per worker, since any increase in investment per worker will be countered by an off-setting diminishment in the return to capital. The level of the growth path is determined by natural endowment and the savings function. However, once the economy is on its long-run steady state growth path faster growth cannot be attained. In the transition to the steady state the economy grows at the same rate as the savings rate until the next plateau where diminishing returns to capital fully offset the increased capital-labor ratio. The Phelps' Golden Rule of Accumulation recommends government policy to raise the savings rate to the level that will maximize consumption over all time. Thus, the Phelps Golden Rule will accelerate economic growth initially, at the cost of current consumption, but the long-run steady state rate of growth cannot be altered.

To reconcile the trade off between present and current consumption turnpike theorems introduced the discount factor into the analysis. Instead of maximizing consumption over all time, as along the golden path, turnpikes assume that economic agents prefer to maximize the present discounted value of consumption over time. Under turnpike theorems, consumption in earlier periods will be greater than on the golden path (since discounting implies greater utility from immediate than from postponed consumption) and the level of the growth path will be lower, yet the long-run steady state rate of growth remains unchanged.

Two sector neo-classical models have been developed by Meade (1961), Uzawa (1961, 1963) and Solow (1961).[5] The main contribution of these models has been to bring greater realism to the neo-classical genre of growth models. Generally, these models include two sectors, one where only a consumption good is produced and the second where only a capital good is produced. The capital good, along with labor and capital, is used in an intermediate step to produce the consumption good. The consumption good can only be consumed. Most of the two sector models assume a classical consumption function (i.e., savings come only from profits), as well as "well-behaved" production functions exhibiting constant returns to scale and diminishing returns to factors.

The two sector models are a contribution perhaps most in that they are the first models to incorporate relative prices. In the two sector model the resultant relative price of capital to consumption good yields the rate of return to capital as well as the equilibrium interest rate paid to savers. The two sector models, once certain restrictions on behavior (such as the capital good industry must be relatively capital intensive, and savings must be proportional to income) yield the much ballyhooed turnpikes, steady states and golden rules that economists of the period enjoyed.

Denison (1985) analyzed trends for the U.S. for 1929-1982, basically confirming the Solow neo-classical model but further differentiating technological progress into: knowledge; resource allocation; economies of scale; and other factors. Quite obviously technological progress remains an area for important research, especially in attempting to explain the sources of long-run economic growth. This was essentially an update of his (1962) analysis, where he accounted for economic growth between 1929-1957. This analysis departed from Solow's treatment of growth, and the neo-classical models, in the way it "accounted" for growth. Denison specified factor inputs according to several breakdowns. He included: growth in employment, impact of shorter hours, work force education, increased experience, and the changing age-sex composition of the work force. He found no contribution from land to economic growth. Capital inputs included: non-farm residential structures, other structures and equipment, and other types of capital. Denison also expected and found increasing returns to capital, resulting, in part, from advances in knowledge, growth of the national market, and growth of local markets. Thus, although Solow could explain less than 30% of economic growth from factor contributions, Denison "explains" 75%, with unaccounted for technological advances as the residual factor. Perhaps most important, Denison's analysis attributes much less importance to the role of reproducible investment in growth than does Solow's and finds a much greater role for improvements in the quality of labor.

While Denison's accounting for growth is quite detailed and provides a series of information and facts that are of use to others developing theories these data might help to confirm or verify, in his own words the growth accounting "neither rests upon nor provides any grand general model or general theory of the ultimate reasons for modern economic growth and variations in growth."[6]   While Denison's accounting indicates major sources of growth in the U.S. economy it does not explain why these determinants of growth occurred as they did. Was it happenstance that knowledge has advanced, why was labor "misallocated" and why was the reallocation of labor a continuing source of growth, and what has been the role of government in these determinants? Denison tells us nothing about why unemployment persists over long periods, although he does account for short-term fluctuations in aggregate demand. In short, Denison provides a thorough and useful accounting of "sources of growth" but deeper causality is not touched upon.

Solow (1970) discusses the "vintage" of capital as another source of growth. In the vintage approach to accounting for growth newer capital investments were more productive than older capital stock. Others[7] would attribute much of technological progress to the accumulation of new capital stock or certain types of capital stock vintage theory holds that even without technological progress new capital investment is more productive than old capital stock, even after accounting for depreciation. In explaining this Solow (1970) uses the case history of a single factory:[8]

> [W]hen it (the factory, that is) is new it earns profits equal to the difference between its productive capacity and its wage bill. As it ages, its productive capacity is unimpaired and its output per man is unchanged. But if, as is normal, the real wage rises through time because of new technological progress and the competition of newer and more efficient factories, its bill will rise and its profits will diminish. Eventually the wage rises as high as the output per man in this factory and it has become the marginal no-rent factory. Let the wage go a touch higher, and this factory goes out of business; it has become obsolete, not because of any reduction in its efficiency, but because the rising real wage has rendered it incapable of covering its own variable costs of production.   (Solow 1970: 47)

The vintage model seems quite plausible, yet none of the empirical work that is surveyed in the next sections have included an indicator of vintage. Anderson (1987) discusses the roles of capital and capital vintage in economic growth but he does not include any estimates of its actual impact on growth.

Summing up: perhaps the clearest points from the neo-classical growth literature are: (1) equilibrium employment and growth are not the stuff of happenstance but are the results of economic forces, (2) it is impossible to "maximize" growth since short-run growth cannot be sustained and can only occur at the cost of reduced current consumption, and (3) an increase in the savings rate will shift the level of the growth path but will not alter the rate of growth of the economy (this can be seen as a transitional change in the growth path of the economy).

Human Capital. Human capital investment is also an important
input into economic growth in many growth models. The new growth
models (the Romer genre discussed below) include human capital as
an important source of externalities and a cause of increasing returns.
Schultz (1963) and Becker (1964) were two of the earliest economists
to include investment in human capital as a major factor in
determining the rate of economic growth.

In 1961, Schultz observed that increases in U.S. national output far
exceeded the increases of land, labor, and capital, and strongly
suggested that the major explanation for the difference could be
accounted for by rapid accumulation of human capital. Schultz argued
that economists had treated all labor as identical without touching
upon differences in the quality of human effort and productivity.
Schultz pointed out that people make very large investments in
themselves, notably, in education, and that if these investments yield
a return that they must be a factor of production that should be
treated as other factors are. Schultz draws on working notes of Gary
Becker to show that investment in education has at least the same
private return as investment in "reproducible capital" and that if half
of what is spent on education is considered to be for consumption
purposes, that the rate of return to human capital (or to education)
is twice that of reproducible capital. Becker (1975) extended his
earlier work in calculating private rates of return to education at
different levels. The rate of return to education was higher, for the
period studied (1939-58), for high school graduates than for college
graduates, indicating a diminishing rate of return with investment in
human capital. Schultz's definition of human capital included:
education, on the job training, health, and migration. Although the
term covers a variety of areas, most of Schultz's effort in measuring
investment in humans has focussed on education, although his policy
implications go beyond education policies. He also observed that the
capital-output ratio had been declining in the U.S. although economic
prosperity continued to advance, indeed, accelerate. Schultz picks no
quarrel with the neo-classical growth model and the implied
diminishing returns but emphasizes that only including "reproducible
capital" in the capital output ratio is incorrect and we should also
include measures of human capital.

Schultz sees an important role for on the job training in increasing
worker productivity. Workers who function in jobs where skills are

not needed or acquired tend to maintain their skills and productivity at low levels, whereas workers who are in functions where skills must be honed experience faster rises in productivity and pay.

Lucas (1988) includes human capital as a source of economic growth. In the Lucas model human capital affects a person's own productivity -- this he refers to as an "internal effect." He also posits that human capital has an "external effect," where the level of human capital raises the productivity of all factors. In this case, the Cobb-Douglas production function is altered:

$$Q=AK^a[Lh]^{1-a}ha\gamma$$

where Q is output
  A is the constant technology level
  K is capital stock
  L is the amount of labor
  h is the stock of human capital raising labor's productivity, and
  haγ is the external effect of human capital on factor
    productivity.

After numerous manipulations of this basic model -- including efforts to explain why if the production of human capital is a linear function of inputs people make their greatest inputs into human capital during their early years -- Lucas applies the model to Denison's estimates of the variables in the model, where Denison calculated human capital in the United States to be growing at an annual average rate of .009. Lucas concludes that this formulation does not fit Denison's data better than Denison's elaboration of the basic Solow model, but it does help explain permanent per capita income differentials across countries.

Barro (1989) includes investment in human capital in his model. In the empirical estimates Barro used the 1960 primary and secondary school enrollment ratios and found a statistically significant positive relationship between growth and human capital as indicated by this proxy. Barro's use of the school enrollment ratios, despite the statistical significance, seems to be a confusion between the stock of human capital and its maintenance (such as the enrollment ratios) versus new investment in human capital (such as increases in the school enrollment ratios over the period of study). Barro's reasoning for using a stock value of human capital was to illustrate that the level of human capital affected growth. Barro also considered government spending on education as a proxy for human capital investment, but found no significant contribution to growth. [9]

Lucas (1988) extends the human capital model to include not only learning in formal settings but also "learning by doing," as did Schultz (1961). Learning by doing is associated with the production of certain goods while formal learning is associated with reduced output to allocate labor time to formal learning. Learning by doing, however, is not costless. Since learning by doing is associated more with the production of some goods than others, its cost is mainly in the reduced choice of consumables. "If different goods are taken to have different potentials for human capital growth, then the same considerations of comparative advantage that determine which goods get produced where will also dictate each country's rate of human capital growth." The introduction of human capital into the model, especially in the form of "learning by doing" allows for persistent differences in growth rates across countries without regard to the differing initial capital levels. Lucas also predicts that countries with higher levels of human capital than others may retain this advantage indefinitely.

Recent Developments. Recent works by Romer (1986, 1989), Easterly and Wetzel (1989), and Easterly (1989) posit increasing returns to scale arising from technological externalities and spillovers from investment in human capital. [10] With increasing returns it is possible to generate economic growth from endogenous variables and to more explicitly investigate some of the policy factors that affect long-run growth.

Romer is a modern pioneer in this approach. In 1986 Romer declared that although increasing returns to scale had already been acknowledged by the economics profession as a reason for the continued pace of economic growth where diminishing returns to factors would have led one to expect slowing growth in the face of constant savings ratios that the approach had nevertheless not been emphasized mainly because of the lack of an empirically relevant model. Romer (1986) presented a "fully specified model of long-run growth in which knowledge is assumed to be an input in production that has increasing marginal productivity."

In Romer's models the rate of increase in technological knowledge, the sector that exhibits increasing returns, is related to the rate of capital accumulation. Thus, because of this externality we should not expect diminishing returns to capital, contrary to the neoclassical model. Yet, in Romer (1989) analysis of cross-country data for developed and developing countries together showed that poorer countries had a higher rate of return to capital and a lower amount of capital available than in richer countries, confirming the conventional models where capital exhibits decreasing returns.

Easterly (1989) presents a theoretical framework for incorporating economic distortions into a Romer-type, increasing returns model. Since Easterly's model is the latest in this type of growth modelling and since it has some direct relevance for the topic of this paper it is discussed below.

Easterly presents a Constant Elasticity of Substitution (CES) model "nested in a Cobb-Douglas" framework.

$$Q = A(1-\gamma)(K_1^{\rho_1}+\gamma K_2^{\rho_2})^{(1-\beta)/\rho_1}L^{\beta}$$

Here, output is a function of the stock of technological knowledge A, two types of capital, K_1 and K_2, and labor L. γ, ρ_1, ρ_2, and β are parameters. The elasticity of substitution between the two types of capital is constant at $1/(\rho 1-1)$. Easterly then introduces a distortion as resulting from tax on one type of capital as opposed to another, which is represented ex post as the ratio of the marginal products of the two capital types:

$$e^t = \frac{\dfrac{\delta Q}{\delta K_1}}{\dfrac{\delta Q}{\delta K_2}}$$

The stock of technological knowledge **A** is a function of the stocks of capital and labor.

In the long run, the stock of knowledge is positively related to the stock of capital, where the stock of capital K is the sum of the two

$$A = \alpha K^{\lambda}L^{\epsilon}$$

forms of capital. α, λ, and ϵ are parameters. This results due to the learning that takes place in the process of investing in physical and human capital, as well as the unintended spillovers to knowledge in areas other than those receiving new investment. In general, innovation and investment respond to fundamentally the same incentives so that in the long-run knowledge is associated with the size of the capital stock.[11] After several manipulations of the basic model, and the distortion figure e^t, and after assuming that labor is constant in the steady state, technological knowledge reduces down to a specific function of the level of capital as weighted by the distortions created by policy in favoring one type of capital over another.

$$Q = \alpha\Phi K$$

and Φ is the affect of the distortion on the accumulation of technical knowledge, since the accumulation of capital is hindered by distortionary taxation.

Easterly's final equation $Q = \alpha\Phi K$ is nearly the same as the Harrod-Domar model for all practical purposes. At a recent seminar given at the World Bank, Romer presented his model and was criticized as not having presented anything more than the Harrod-Domar model with a few bells and whistles. I suggest a simplification of the model and emphasize that the model behaves differently in the short- to intermediate-run than it does in the longer-run. The difference between short to intermediate and longer term is important for without the distinction the endogenous growth models appear to suffer the same "knife edge" of instability as the earlier Harrod-Domar models did.

In the simplified version there are two factors of production, K and L. Additionally, the level of technology at any given point in time is fixed and is indicated by A. In a Cobb-Douglas production function we can write:

$$Q = AK^{\alpha}L^{1-\alpha}, \text{ where } 0 < \alpha < 1,$$

which in the short- to intermediate-run, with only A fixed (the short- to intermediate-run is long enough for both capital and labor to change, although we will assume from here that the labor force does not grow) is linear homogeneous exhibiting constant returns to scale, since

$$\alpha + 1 - \alpha = 1.$$

However, if A is a function of the level of capital stock, such as

$$A = K^\lambda, \text{ where } \lambda > 0$$

and is allowed to vary over the longer run, then the production function can be rewritten

$$Q = K^\lambda K^\alpha L^{1-\alpha},$$

which exhibits increasing returns to scale,
since $\lambda + \alpha + 1 - \alpha = \lambda + 1 > 0$.

Looking at changes in the short term production function

$$Q = AK^\alpha L^{1-\alpha},$$

letting capital accumulate but assuming no
growth in labor

$$\delta^2 Q/\delta K^2 = A(\alpha - 1)\alpha K^{\alpha-2} L^{1-\alpha}$$

but the second derivative indicates diminishing returns to capital in the short run,

$$\frac{\delta^2 Q}{\delta K^2} = A(\alpha - 1)\alpha K^{\alpha-2} L^{1-\alpha} < 0$$

since $(\alpha - 1) < 0$.

However, in the longer run, with increasing returns to scale and

$$Q = K^\lambda K^\alpha L^{1-\alpha} = K^{\lambda+\alpha} L^{1-\alpha}$$

the marginal product of capital, again with labor held constant,

$$\frac{\delta Q}{\delta K} = (\lambda+\alpha)^{\lambda+\alpha-1} L^{1-\alpha} > 0,$$

and

$$\frac{\delta^2 Q}{\delta K^2} = (\lambda+\alpha)(\lambda+\alpha-1)^{\lambda+\alpha-2} L^{1-\alpha}$$

which if $\lambda+\alpha > 1$, will also be positive.

This implies that in the short- to intermediate-run, as in the Solow model, an increase in the capital-labor ratio will lead to an increase in output per laborer, however, the rate of increase diminishes as the capital-labor ratio increases. Over the longer term, the rate of increase in the output per worker ratio need not decline if the stock of technological knowledge rises sufficiently to offset the usual law of variable proportions, that is, if λ is greater than 1-α. This shows, that even if we have increasing returns to scale, this does not necessarily imply that there will not be diminishing returns to factors, and, the rate of technological improvement (now endogenously determined by the rate of capital accumulation) remains the key to continued growth in per capita incomes.

Both Easterly's and Romer's models provide significant contributions to understanding the transition to the long-run steady state. Both models essentially rely on the increasing returns that arise from externalities and spillovers from investment into the stock of technical knowledge. Such accumulation of technological knowledge must occur over an extended period. Easterly assumes technological knowledge flows across borders, which in the intermediate term may have a much more powerful an effect on growth than endogenously determined levels of technological knowledge, implying that countries that invest only a little still may achieve economic growth through the importation of technological knowledge.

Some Empirical Evidence.[12] This section presents some of the empirical evidence of the impact on growth of: government spending and taxation, trade orientation, financial sector development, and a number of other variables, such as price instability and population growth.

A very large number of studies have included government as a determinant of the rate of economic growth.[13] In most instances a negative relationship between the size of government and economic growth is found. Most explanations of this negative relationship refer to the incentives distorting aspects of taxation. In Barro (1989) taxation leads to distortions in resource use and hence slows growth, while certain expenditures, in particular, expenditures on human capital as well as physical capital (infrastructure) investment, have positive impact on economic growth.

Gemmel (1983) finds an inverse relationship between government size and economic growth, consistent with the rest of the literature where the size of government and concordant taxation hinder resource use. However, he finds a positive relationship between economic growth and growth in government, consistent with the Keynesian model of demand management. Neither Landau (1986) nor Barro (1989a&b) find a positive relationship between the ratio of government spending on education and economic growth. This may be due to the way they specify investment in human capital.[14]

Kormendi and Meguire (1985) find no statistically significant relationship between the change in the ratio of government to GDP and economic growth. Grier and Tullock (1989) using the growth in the share of government consumption in GDP (growth in the ratio) find a negative impact on growth for a larger sample of countries.

Easterly (1989) provides a framework for reconciling the contradictory positive impact of government spending and the negative impact of taxation on economic growth. Government spending provides for useful, growth inducing investment in social overhead capital, supports investment in human capital and provides public goods. The marginal contribution of such spending to economic growth diminishes. At the same time, such spending must be financed. If we assume it is entirely financed through taxation then if the marginal negative impact of taxation on economic growth is also diminishing there will be some optimal size of government, that indicated by (B) in Figure 2.1.

In the Easterly model government taxes are imposed on one form of capital but not on others. This creates a distortion, where the marginal product of one type of capital is greater than that of another. The higher is taxation the greater the distortion and, since distortions slow growth, the slower economic growth. On the other hand, government provision of public goods and investment, such as all education spending as well as investment in social overhead capital, leads to economic growth. In Figure 2.1 there are no deficits, all expenditures[15] are covered by tax revenues. Government "saving" represents a certain fixed portion of tax revenues. Hence, a higher government saving rate stimulates greater economic growth for the same level of taxation.

As taxes rise as a share of GDP their marginal, negative impact on GDP rises, too. Similarly, as government expenditure rises the marginal benefit such spending has for stimulating growth declines.

Easterly assumes, for simulation purposes, that government saves and invests a fixed portion of tax revenues with the rest going to current consumption of public and merit goods. At point A there is no taxation. As government raises the rate of taxation economic growth accelerates, fueled by productive public sector investment. Growth reaches a maximum at B, where the marginal return to public sector investment just equals the marginal negative effect of taxation.[16] Increasing the rate of tax imposition, resulting in a movement from point B to C, causes a deceleration of economic growth because the distortionary negative impact of higher taxes outweighs the marginal growth from further public investment. To the left of point C any attempt to raise the rate of tax imposition so much swamps the impact of continued public investment that both lower economic growth and lower tax revenues result, with a lower effective tax rate (i.e., tax/GDP), ex post. From C to the origin nominal tax rate increases are entirely counterproductive in terms of revenue and economic growth.

Easterly posits that "revenue maximizing" or "patronage maximizing" states will seek to attain point C, while "benevolent, growth maximizing" states will seek to attain point B. He posits that most states fall between these two polar positions and therefore most

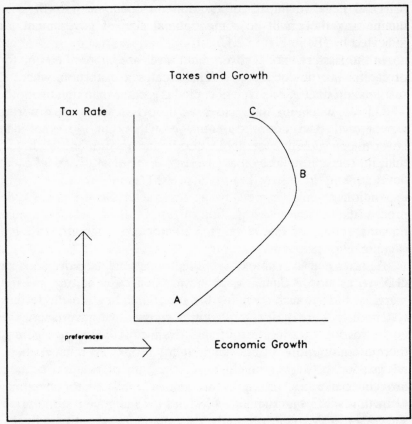

Figure 2.1

observations between economic growth and tax rates will fall between B and C, a negatively sloped segment.

A number of authors have pointed out relationships between trade policy (or trade orientation) and economic growth, for instance, Edwards (1988a), World Bank (1987), and Ram (1985). The research generally supports the notion that openness, or an outward trade orientation, is positively related to economic growth. The arguments made are that trade openness leads to improved resource allocation (due to the imperative of international competition) and from reduced rent-seeking. Improved resource allocation or reduced rent-seeking are assumed rather than measured or estimated. Exports are sometimes seen as a factor that leads to the greater diffusion of technology and benefits from scale economies.

In general, outward orientation is positively related to economic growth in most of the literature of the 1970s and 1980s. The reasons proffered vary and even causality is questioned, yet the statistical relationship does exist.

Development of financial institutions, instruments and their unrepressed operation are seen to lead to economic growth.[17] However, Jung (1986), applying Granger-Sims causality tests concludes that in some instances financial development leads to economic development, in others economic development leads to financial innovations, while in still others financial system development proceeds in tandem with general economic development. In any case, financial repression (say as evinced by negative real rates of interest) is generally seen to be deleterious to growth.

Easterly and Wetzel (1989) list a number of works, which they describe as mostly anecdotal, relating institutional development and administration to economic development. Among these are a stable system of civil liberties, defense, law and order, and property rights.[18]

In Kormendi and Meguire (1985) a series of macroeconomic theories of structure, policies and growth are tested using regression analysis for forty-seven countries. They find a negative relationship between per capita income level and the rate of growth, which is consistent with neoclassical theory and diminishing returns to capital. They also found population growth to be positively related to GDP growth but with a coefficient less than unitary and so implying faster growing populations will experience slower growth in per capita GDP, cet. par. The variability in money growth (indicated by the standard deviation of money supply shocks) also leads to slower growth, confirming a hypothesis related to rational expectations. They found little direct relationship between export orientation and growth, but a strong relationship to investment. Kormendi and Meguire use a series of indicators as tests of various hypotheses, however, they present no overall macroeconomic growth model to explain how or why these varied indicators should be included in a single regression nor whether or not they may be related to each other.

Grier and Tullock (1989) present essentially the same type of analysis as Kormendi and Meguire but for a larger sample of countries and using a model that allows for temporal and cross-country stability of coefficients. Their results are similar to Kormendi and Meguire's except, interestingly, they find mixed support for convergence, i.e., the coefficient for per capita income was not negative, and they find little significant about inflation and inflation variability. Interestingly, Grier and Tullock confirm the convergence hypothesis for OECD countries but not for developing countries. They also find that population growth has no clear relationship with GDP growth in Africa nor in Asia. Grier and Tullock (1989) do not take a formal approach to growth. Instead they "investigate empirical regularities" in economic growth, without reference to a single, specific model.

Barro (1989) uses the Cobb-Douglas model and incorporates increasing returns, which result when population growth is endogenized and investment in human capital is an exogenous variable. Barro includes government taxation as a distortion in the model, while government investment is a proxy for increase in the stock of public, physical infrastructure. Barro also includes an indicator of political rights (Gastil, 1987), which he assumes is a good proxy for economic (property) rights. Barro uses average data for the period 1960-1985 for 72 countries, with dummy variables representing Africa and Latin America. He explains that these two regional dummy variables are proxies for aspects of political instability and government restrictions on trade. But, we already know that these two regions experienced less economic growth than the rest of the world during this period.[19] Perhaps this serves to raise the statistical "goodness of fit" of his regressions but it does little to explain differences in economic growth.[20]

Summary. Keynesian growth models are optimistic. Investment can lead to growth and insufficient investment can be supplemented by government investment and foreign savings. In the Harrod-Domar models there is no stable equilibrium between per capita output, labor force growth, and full employment. Instead, full employment occurs either as a matter of luck or as a result of government policies. In the steady state of neo-classical growth output cannot grow faster than population. But, the neo-classical model is optimistic in that it does not allow for declining output per worker. The only way declining output per worker could occur is if capital per worker were to decline. But a decline in capital per worker is not sustainable since at lower levels of capital per worker the return to investment is higher thus spurring new investment. Additionally, the neo-classical model, by assuming a production function that includes substitution between capital and labor, sees full employment as a stable equilibrium as a result of economic forces rather than the "knife edge" happenstance of the Harrod-Domar model.

The economic growth literature in some instances touches upon efficient use of capital, or resources in general, yet, it does not explicitly incorporate allocative efficiency into estimated growth models. The role of the state, or more precisely, the size of government, has been included in many of the cross-sectional empirical works, while the nature of the state has only recently been discussed, although the implications of the state's nature have not yet been empirically tested. The next logical steps include a model which explicitly incorporates how resources are used to produce economic goods and the role of the state in this process.

Rent-Seeking

In the next several pages, summarizing the rent-seeking literature, I discuss the meaning of rent-seeking, how rents are harvested, competitive and efficient rent-seeking, and the social costs of rent-seeking. As rent-seeking refers to the direct use or waste of economic resources for non-economic gains this literature provides a basis for addressing some of the failings of the economic growth literature.

The Meaning of Rent-Seeking. A narrow view of rent-seeking embraces activities designed to capture rents or scarcity premia that accrue to holders of licenses, quotas and the like. Typical examples include lobbying that aims to secure import licenses in trade or allocations of foreign exchange in systems where it is allocated outside the market process. Lobbies seek to restrict foreign competition, regulate industry, shift taxation (for instance, implicit taxation of the agricultural sector), regulate foreign exchange, etc. These lobbies in each instance entail the use of resources that aim to transfer income from some group to others, for example, from farmers to city dwellers or from consumers to importers. Rent-seeking also occurs without government intervention. For instance, the strikes of unionized workers seek to transfer income from management and consumers to labor.

Ekelund and Tollison (1981 and 1984) explain rent-seeking waste as the expenditure of resources devoted toward the achievement of rent, where the loss to society is not only the usual dead-weight loss triangle but also the costs of lobbying, investment in over-capacity, over investment in human capital to secure civil service positions, smuggling, etc. In their study of the mercantilist era in Europe they show that society wasted resources through the creation of rent opportunities through regulation of internal and external trade. Bhagwati's (1982) concept of "directly unproductive profit-seeking" is more comprehensive, and includes all means of gaining profit through the use of resources without adding to the stock of goods and services. For instance, to Ekelund and Tollison's calculations, Bhagwati adds welfare improving but directly unproductive activities within the context of second-best policies. Activities which seek to remove distortionary policies, such as lobbying by consumers who wish to purchase imports without paying high duties, use resources without adding to the stock of goods and services, but are welfare improving since they seek to reduce distortion. Bhagwati also includes a very similar but somewhat distinct type of rent-seeking, which he calls "revenue-seeking." Revenue-seeking refers to the resource using activities that government undertakes for purely legitimate revenue generation, such as taxation. While revenue-seeking can refer to all activities meant to increase government revenues most attention has focused on indirect taxes, especially import duties.

Rent-seeking should not be confused with profit-seeking. New technology, a recently opened market, or the discovery of natural resources in an advantageous location relative to their market all offer above market returns to factors. Indeed, entrepreneurial activities that are attracted to these rents should not be confused with rent-seeking. It is precisely these sort of rents that attract new economic activity, and with competition these rents will be competed away. Such rents generate new and productive activity and add to national product. Should entrepreneurs, however, take actions to limit the entry of competition for these rents, such as lobbying government to issue licenses, this type of activity seeks to maintain rents yet does not yield production. In short, "Rent-Seeking is the expenditure of scarce resources to capture an artificially[21] created transfer." (Tollison 1982)

Baldwin (1984) offers a typology of ways rents can be harvested (or captured), particularly by the capitalists and workers involved in import competing or in export industries. These include:

1. An import competing industry will seek protection against competing imports through seeking to have government impose tariffs;
2. An exporting industry is more likely to seek government provided subsidies;
3. Capitalists in both sectors will also lobby government for access to subsidized capital, either below market rates or as 'outright grant;'
4. Import competing industry may often prefer to seek quotas since the impact is often more predictable. (Tariffs can encourage profit cutting by foreign competitors.) These firms may find less resistance from countervailing foreign lobbyists, who may prefer quotas or VERs (voluntary export restraints), since foreign firms fortunate enough to be allotted quotas will usually reap most of the windfall cartelization gains.

Bhagwati (1982) a typology of directly-unproductive activities, examples and consequences, drawing upon the works of others and his own. These either give rise to economic distortions or result from economic distortions (which we assume were generated by rent-seeking in the first place). These activities, seeking to gain rents, premia or revenue, or to maintain such or avoid the negative incidence of such, are either legal or illegal. They either have the consequence of immiserizing society, or may paradoxically improve society from a second-best (or worse) position. All of these activities, at any rate, on an overall basis, result in immiserization. Some of the examples Bhagwati provides[22] include:

1. Monopoly seeking lobbying (legal)
2. Tariff evasion or smuggling (illegal)
3. Theft (illegal)
4. Tariff seeking lobbying (legal)
5. Tariff destroying lobbying with aid of bribes to politicians (legal and illegal).

Social Costs. Social costs of monopoly, when examined by Harberger (1954) were seen to be trivial. Harberger assumed, consistent with received theory, that the only cost of monopoly was that referred to as "dead weight loss" triangle, see Figure 2.2. The rent-seeking literature pointed out however, that if rent-seeking is competitive the entire rent (area R) would be competed away in wasteful activities seeking to capture the rent. Thus the rent-seeking related cost of monopoly would be area R while the standard dead weight loss would still represent the misallocative loss to society. Therefore total monopoly social cost would comprise both R and D, i.e., C=R+D, where C is the total social cost of monopoly.

Posner (1975) calculated the dead weight loss triangle to be approximately equal to $D = 1/2dPdQ$ and the rent, $R = dP(Q-Q_c)$, where Q_c refers to the quantity of output that would have prevailed under conditions of competitive markets. Posner then illustrates the relative "smallness" of D compared to R, dividing D by R

$$D/R = 1/2dPdQ/dP(Q-Q_c)$$

$$= dQ/2(Q-dQ),$$

which can be expressed in terms of the elasticity of demand for the product at the competitive price (e) and the percentage increase in price brought about by monopolization (ρ):

$$D/R = \frac{\dfrac{1}{2dPdQ}}{dP(Q-Q_c)} = \frac{dq}{2(Q-dQ)}$$

and

$$\partial(D/R)/\partial e = 2\rho/(2-2\rho e)^2 > 0;$$

$$\partial(D/R)/\partial\rho = 2e/(2-2\rho e)^2 > 0;$$

Which is to say that the ratio of D to R is smaller the less elastic the demand for the product at the competitive price and the smaller the percentage price increase over the competitive price level.

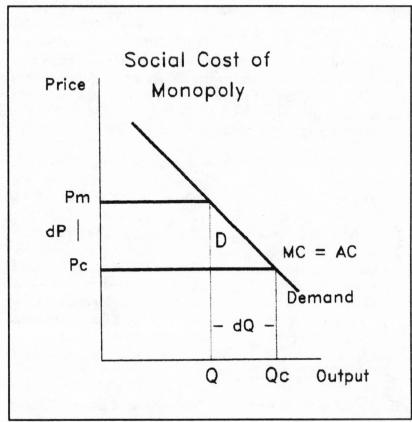

Figure 2.2

Using this basic relationship, or ratio D to R, and working from Harberger's analysis, Posner calculates that instead of monopoly having social costs of .1 percent of US GNP, with D/R = .03, the more likely value would be approximately 3.3 percent of GNP. The analysis is very sensitive to estimates of (e) and (ρ) but the differences between D and L remain great, assuming D to be the social cost of monopoly when there is in fact competitive rent-seeking will underestimate the social cost of monopoly by several orders of magnitude.

Competitive Rent-Seeking. Krueger (1974) illustrates the competition related to rent-seeking through the competition for import licenses that takes place among potential importers under a trade regime entailing quantitative restrictions. Relying upon an example given by Bhagwati and Desai (1970) Krueger explains how importers will invest in over-capacity in order to gain import licenses up to the point where the marginal additional cost (opportunity cost of investing elsewhere) of over-capacity is equal to the marginal rent received through being allowed to import the licensed good. The case of the licensing of imported intermediate goods is illustrated:

> When licenses are allocated in proportion to firms' capacities, investment in additional physical plant confers upon the investor a higher expected receipt of import licenses. Even with initial excess capacity (due to quantitative restrictions upon imports of intermediate goods), a rational entrepreneur may still expand his plant if the expected gains from the additional import licenses he will receive, divided by the cost of the investment, equal the returns on investment in other activities. This behavior would be perfectly rational even if, for all entrepreneurs, the total number of import licenses remains fixed. ... By investing in additional capacity, entrepreneurs devote resources to compete for import licenses. (Krueger 1974: 292-3)

Krueger makes the same cases for the licensing of imported consumer goods and less formal allocations that lead to (or are greased by) bribery.

Bribery had usually been treated as a transfer, and therefore not welfare reducing. However, Krueger points out that if bribes are a part of the remuneration system for officials then there will be competition for government jobs. This competition can take place in training or obtaining educational requirements for meeting government job prerequisites.

For most any type of rent, Krueger sums up, "If all individuals choose their activities on the basis of expected returns, rates of returns on alternative activities will be equated and, in that sense, markets will be competitive." This leads to the conclusion that all rents will eventually be "competed away" through competitive rent seeking.

So far, it has been assumed that competitive rent-seeking leads to an "efficient" outcome, i.e., where the rate of return to rent-seekers is equalized to the rate of return to other, more productive, economic activities. There are other ways of looking at the process. Tullock (1980b) discusses how rent-seeking may quite simply not yield the same rate of return of other activities. There is little reason to expect that rent-seeking can benefit from economies of scale (for instance, big lobbyists are unlikely to be more successful relative to their size than are little lobbyists). Also, there is no reason to expect that rent-seekers should have identical efficiencies, i.e., there need not be any shake out of less efficient rent-seekers as economic theory posits for competitive firms producing homogeneous products. Where rent-seeking is not competitive marginal costs of factor inputs will be less than marginal returns from rent-seeking. If the productive sector is more competitive the marginal return to rent-seeking may exceed the marginal return to productive factor use.

Tullock (in both the 1980b and 1975 articles) discusses rent-seeking (or the winning of court cases) based upon a probabilistic lottery process. To the extent that rent-seeking can be seen as a lottery process and where the number of competitors in the process has an impact on the probability of the returns not in direct proportion to the size of the returns competitive rent-seeking might be expected to lead to greater waste of resources than less competitive processes. Indeed, Tullock's intention is to assist in designing processes that minimize rent competition and hence reduce waste of resources.

Given the importance of the Tullock model for subsequent works the basic structure is presented here.

If the probability of winning a rent (like winning a lottery) is equal to the ratio of a rent-seeker's participation (or lottery player's) in the competition to the total amount of rent-seeking competition (total number of lottery tickets sold) then the probability of winning the rent can be expressed:

$$P_A = \frac{A^r}{A^r + B^r}$$

Where P_A is the probability of A winning the rent (lottery prize), A is the amount of resources A has devoted to rent-seeking, B is the amount of resources devoted to rent-seeking by A's competitor B. r is an exponent. In the case that the probability function is linear r=1. In all other cases r ≠ 1.

Taking the linear case the simple solution might appear that the entire amount of rent available will just equal the amount of resources that A and B will be willing to squander on its attainment. This is incorrect.

If the total rent equals $100 and A spends $50 on seeking the rent while B spends $25 on seeking the rent then A's expected value of the "investment" is equal to (50/75)*$100 = $66.67 and B's is equal to $33.33. For both parties the percentage increase in expected value over rent waste is the same. However, if A should instead invest only $40 this reduction of investment of $10 would only result in a reduction of expected value to $61.53, with an increase in B's expected value. Thus, by investing $10 less A's net worth increases by about $5. In the case of collusion A and B can spend a total of $1 (one ticket purchase in the lottery) and split the net winnings of $99.

In Tullock (1980b, Tables 6.1 and 6.2) various scenarios are presented. In the simple linear probability case Tullock shows that in the limit (i.e., with the number of rent competitors approaching infinite) the total amount that will be wasted on rent-seeking is about equal to the total amount of rent available. In all cases, i.e., whether the exponent r is greater than, less than or equal to one {r>1≥r}, as the number of competitors rises the amount wasted on rent-seeking also rises. And, when r>1 total rent-seeking waste may exceed total available rent, while when r<1 total rent available will likely exceed the amount wasted on rent-seeking.

From this analysis Tullock draws two conclusions. The first is that the numbers competing for rents should be limited. The second is that the return to rent-seeking should also be limited. The return to rent-seeking here is the exponent r. For instance, if cramming for a civil service exam (a waste of resources in this instance) has a high likely payoff (r will be large) then resources will be wasted on cramming. If instead cramming will not increase a test taker's likelihood of passing the exam then test takers will not spend their energies on taking exams. In short, Tullock recommends rent competitions that are limited in the sense that only few may participate (participation may be restricted to members of certain groups, such as family, clan, ethnic group, tribe, sexual persuasion, etc.). Also, competition among the limited participants should be geared toward wasting as few resources as possible. Rents should be meted out swiftly and arbitrarily.

Congleton (1980) also discusses competition for rents in terms of game theory, where two competitors, Robinson Crusoe and Friday on a dessert island, vie for "Winner Take All That Remains." In this situation "If neither Friday nor Crusoe has a particular advantage in the initial distribution of wealth or in ability to deploy wealth for attack or defense, then the victor will be that individual who devotes most of his wealth to 'attack.'"

The game is then extended to include an arbitrator, the addition of the arbitrator leads to a Pareto more efficient allocation than without, but both cases are second-best. The game is extended one further, to the competitive game in a majority rule state. Under majority rule, rent-seeking, through the purchase of support, will entail even more efficient allocation of resources since, with non-pure strategies, coalitions can be bought for less than the amount of resources that would have to be devoted to the purpose under either of the previous two games. Congleton does not make the facile case that competition must improve resource use but he does conclude that "institutions can, at least in highly simplified circumstances, create incentives for individuals to use less wasteful or even productive competitive means. Under "both" game formats,[23] it proved possible to shift from competitive methods that consumed resources to ones that merely transferred them (e.g., the shift from anarchy to a single arbitrator changed the competitive means from warfare to bribery and generated a Pareto-superior state.)"

Millner and Pratt (1989) take the analysis one step further by the design and implementation of a lottery type experiment with graduate students as white mice. The conclusion basically confirms Tullock's view that institutions can determine how much waste is associated with rent-seeking. Tullock's equation for a two rent-seeker model is

$$A = rX/4,$$

where A is the optimal rent-seeking expenditure for
    individual A,
      r is derived from the probabilistic returns equation
      and is related to institutional arrangements,

X is the monopoly profit (or transfer, or any other
kind of rent).

Millner and Pratt conclude from their experiments that their "...
results lend support to Tullock's argument that social welfare is
protected by adopting institutions which lower the exponent (r)..."
Such institutional arrangements that would lower r and hence reduce
rent-seeking waste would be where "it is better if the political
appointments of corrupt governments are made quickly and rather
arbitrarily." (Tullock prefers politicians to appoint bureaucrats rather
than having potential bureaucrats cram for entrance exams for civil
service positions.)

Michaels (1988) points out that where politicians have monopoly
power in the provision of a particular resource (he calls it capital)
needed for rent-seeking, a monopoly price for the resource will be
charged. Where Tullock's model could lead to the conclusion that as
the number of rent-seekers increases the expenditure per individual
rent-seeker decreases although overall rent-seeking expenditure
(waste) will increase. This is derived from:

$$\frac{(N-1)Wr}{N^2}$$

which is the individual rent-seeker's total
expenditure, where
    N is the number of rent-seekers,
    W is total amount of rent being sought,
    r is the Tullock exponent mentioned earlier.[24]
Michaels then assumes that there is a fixed cost to becoming a rent-
seeker, perhaps a registration fee, which can be represented by F.
The maximization problem for the monopolist politician is:

$$(\frac{Max}{N}) \frac{N-1}{N} Wr - NF$$

the solution of which is:

$$N^* = \frac{Wr}{F}(1/2)$$

Thus, "the optimal number of seekers to allow increases with the size of total rents and the size of the Tullock exponent."

To the extent the politician is the only producer of the rent-seeking capital (say, the politician is a dictator) the number of rent-seekers will be limited, but their per unit rent expenditure will be higher. The converse may be that where politicians must compete in providing rent-seekers with this special capital the total amount of resources wasted on rent-seeking may be greater although the unit cost may be lower.

Michaels serves the literature well by bringing institutional analysis into what had been looked at mainly from the perspective of games or lotteries. The objectives of the politician must be included in our analysis of rent-seeking as should the market power of the politician. Michaels' efforts, however, neglect other aspects. For instance, to the extent the politician maintains a monopoly on the specific type of capital the politician may also offer greater certainty of gaining rent. Hence the capital discussed may be more valuable since its productivity is more certain.

Hillman and Katz (1984) derive a model incorporating risk aversion, where if rents are "large" the amounts which an individual firm, under competitive rent-seeking, is prepared to expend in rent-seeking diminishes. Also, rent dissipation declines as risk aversion increases. On the other hand, their model indicates that dissipation of rents is incomplete if rent-seeking is not competitive even if rent-seekers are risk-neutral. In general, the literature on efficient rent-seeking tends to indicate that several factors affect how much rent-seeking takes place. These factors include: the number of rent-seekers involved, their attitudes toward risk, the size and probabilistic returns to rent-seeking, and the institutional arrangements that distribute rents, e.g., "winner take all that remains," or "proportional shares." To a large extent the theoretical literature is based on games and improbable situations (lotteries and dessert islands). The games, somehow, are unsatisfactory in their lack of semblance to reality. To extend the field of knowledge in the most useful manner it is necessary to apply concepts of competitive and efficient rent-seeking to analysis of existing, differentiated institutional arrangements.

   Rent-Seeking and Groups. Rent-seeking, as all economic activities, will be pursed most vigorously when returns are highest relative to returns elsewhere. Why do some people, or groups, tend toward rent-seeking more than other groups? Why do some people pursue an activity more than other people? Perhaps differences in talent can explain this. Maybe certain ethnic groups have greater talent at rent-seeking than have other groups, perhaps not. Olson (1989) refers to the predilection toward violence among individuals (or groups) under anarchy, while Reid (1988) refers to the ability to "articulate" under political systems.

   Orr (1980) discusses the rent-seeking of the elderly in the United States. He points out that a factor affecting individual participation in rent-seeking (and, in particular, in seeking pure transfers) is the numerical size of the group or interest that seeks to enlist the individual in the pursuit of transfers. If the group size is too small its voting block, or other form of power, may be insufficient to have its interest prevail within a democratic or pluralistic society. A very small group may not have the geographic representation that would be required. On the other hand, if the group is too large the benefit claims of transferees may be too numerous in relation to the size of the potential benefit they would receive to make organization and rent-seeking activities worthwhile. Or, if the benefit they would receive is large relative to the wealth of society they will be strongly opposed.

   Mbaku and Paul (1989) attempt to associate rent-seeking with political instability. Their empirical analysis investigates the willingness to attempt coups d'etat with some very poorly specified indicators of rent-seeking in Africa.[25] The article indicates a significant relationship between the homogeneity of a country's population and political instability. This statistical relationship, though, may tell very little about rent-seeking but does indicate a social determinant of political instability. To the extent political instability affects investor confidence, people's ability to plan, and their perceptions of risk, a lack of homogeneity can be expected to lead to slower economic growth.

Olson (1983) presents a theory of growth where the influence of special interest groups "reduce the rate of growth along with the level of income where they (interest groups) use their power to block innovation. Olson presents a number of poignant examples, and further empirical evidence is provided by Choi (1983) to support this hypothesis in democratic countries. On this basis one would expect the prevalence of interest groups to result in slower economic growth. Olson does a very poor job of considering the competition among interest groups and how such competition might alter his conclusions.[26]

<u>Rent-Seeking and Growth.</u> It has generally be supposed that while rent-seeking may lower the level of output it generally would not affect the growth of output. Tullock (1984) says that while the US economy, upon independence, inherited an economic system riddled with regulation which resulted in lower welfare than otherwise, the US economy, nevertheless, enjoyed considerable growth at the time.[27] Lucas (1987) points out that while the centrally planned economies of Eastern Europe suffer from severe misallocations and resultant reduced welfare and output they have experienced economic growth at least comparable to that enjoyed in Western industrialized countries. Certainly Tullock and Lucas have not had the last word on this.

Murphy, Schleifer and Vishny (1990) consider the allocation of talent, increasing returns to "super stars", relative returns (private vs. social returns) and implications for economic growth. In their model the most able people choose occupations that exhibit increasing returns to ability. The model then holds that "rent-seeking activities often attract the best and the brightest because they have the weakest diminishing returns to scale."[28] Murphy et al. maintain that rent-seeking is a field with weakly diminishing returns. In their model rent-seeking is mainly concerned with transfers of wealth rather than reaping a slice of current spending. Since wealth is much greater than current spending the size of the rent market is much larger. Ergo, returns to rent-seekers are likely to exceed, at the super star level, returns to entrepreneurship. While an entrepreneur may capture initial rents these rents will soon be whittled away by competition. The authors also argue that the work of engineers and inventors are difficult to fully compensate since the value of their output is embodied in the work of others. For lawyers and traders, however, earnings are easily quantified and these professionals can then negotiate for a larger share of their contribution to profits. In contrast, for inventors and engineers to earn closer to the value of their input they need to become entrepreneurs.

The implications for growth are that if the most able people earn their livings as rent-seekers then we can expect lower levels of income, whereas if more people move into entrepreneurial areas then we can expect higher levels of income. The larger the rent-seeking sector the larger a tax it imposes on the productive sectors and weakens incentives. Also, if less talent moves to the entrepreneurial sector there will be less invention, innovation, technological progress and hence less growth.

The empirical test of the model takes the proportion of university students in law as an indication of the relative attractiveness of the rent-seeking sector. The proportion of engineering students, on the other hand, indicates the relative private return to entrepreneurial, productive activities. These two indicators are then tacked on to Barro's data set (1989) for two sub-sets, one consisting of 55 countries (where the number of university students exceed 10,000) and 91 countries (all available data), where growth in real GDP per capita is the dependent variable. For the 91 country set they find the coefficient for the engineering indicator to be significantly greater than zero and for lawyering it is significantly less than zero, both in conformity with the model. For the 55 country data sub-set, however, the engineering coefficient changed sign but was not significant, and the coefficient for lawyering becomes closer to zero (i.e., less negative) and insignificant.

There are other, more traditional, explanations for the signs of these coefficients. To some extent lawyers can be seen to battle over present wealth. Where wealth is greater we should expect to find more lawyers. With diminishing returns to capital then slower growth would be associated with incentives to work as lawyers since lawyering is in greater demand where there is more wealth. Additionally, where capital accumulation is not far advanced, returns to capital, technology, and innovation may be greater. In such case, returns to engineering would be greater.

Ekelund and Tollison (1981) relate the competition among state institutions to the costs and uncertainties facing would be rent-seekers.

They posit that greater competition, such as in more democratic states, will impose higher costs of rent-seeking compared to the less democratic states. Thus, in the more democratic state (they use England of 200 years ago) there will be less rent-seeking and greater growth than in the less democratic (France of the same era). The Ekelund and Tollison model is the basis of the extended theory of rent-seeking and is fully discussed in the next chapter.

Summary. A few important inferences can be drawn from this mass of literature:

1. the social cost of monopoly and regulation is much greater than the deadweight triangle;
2. how great the social cost is depends upon how much rents are dissipated through competition;
3. less competitive rent-seeking processes seem to indicate a lower social cost of rent-seeking, although more rent-seeking is likely to occur and more distortions might be expected;
4. most of the literature on the efficiency of rent-seeking has dealt with the issue through game theoretic or probability functions, it is time to further consider the institutional arrangements that lead to rent dissipation;
5. dealing with institutional arrangements regarding the dissipation of rents implies the need for a stylized theory of the state.

The next section discusses briefly the role of the state in recent growth models as well as the recent literature on the "New Political Economy" and its applicability to developing countries.

The State and Economic Growth[29]

Early development economics held an unquestioning faith in the ability of the state to correct market failures and to effectively direct the economic process toward development goals. After several decades of experience the literature has now come full circle. A rebirth of neo-classicism and accounting of "government failure" predominates the literature. The neo-classical economists emphasize the transaction costs and imperfect information problems being as great for government as for private decision makers.

This section discusses some competing theories of the role of the state in development, some empirical evidence relating the degree of democracy to economic growth, the role of an independent judiciary as a state institution and how its independence affects the likelihood that rules and regulations (and rents) are enforced, and a brief discussion of the relevance or irrelevance for development of the "new political economy" and its view of the state.

Competing Theories. Much of the debate has been conducted in a political vacuum. Economists often point out ways of improving efficiency, accumulation or income distribution but governments are often slow to implement these recommendations, or indeed work in opposite manner. Marxists are usually more forthcoming in spelling out their theory of the state. But they usually see the state as solely an instrument of a class against the rest of society. Or in more recent times they see the state as having "relative autonomy" and working on behalf of the dominant class rather than on its behest.

In recent neoclassical theories of the state the state is often passive, where the state responds to rent-seeking behavior of various groups and lobbies. This new neoclassical emphasis is on the wastage of resources. The waste is measured as the deviation from competitive or pareto optimum. Bardhan (1988) sees this as a problem since the alternative to this sub-optimal situation is not necessarily Pareto optimal either. Bardhan has developed the case of the large and heterogeneous coalition of dominant classes using collective action as a means of frittering away the country's investible surplus in the form of public subsidies and indifferent management of public investment, resulting in slow industrial growth.

Bardhan points out that none of the existing theories of the state provides a satisfactory general theoretical explanation of how different interventionist states with command over roughly similar instruments of control end up being a developmental state in some cases (e.g., South Korea) as opposed to a primarily regulatory one in some others (e.g., India) or for that matter evolve from a preoccupation with zero-sum rent-seeking (in Korea under Rhee) to a dynamic entrepreneurial state (Korea under Park or Chun).

Relevant to the theory of the state and the state's role in the development process is discussion of the role and feasibility of democracy in development. Three major theories[30] have been rather tenacious in their staying power. First is the theory that perceives democracy as a form of government likely only in market or capitalist economies. A second views democracy as more likely to be sustained in wealthy or economically developed societies. Finally, a third, posits that well established political traditions of compromise politics and of checks and balances on central power help countries evolve into democracies. Kohli melds these three facets into one; suggesting that democracy is most likely to take hold in wealthy capitalist countries with traditions of "proto-democracy."

In short, Kohli sees democracy as coincident with capitalism. Although this is not to imply that capitalism is a necessary and sufficient condition for democracy to take hold. For instance, Argentina, Brazil and Korea are all capitalist countries but certainly not paradigms of democracy, although democratic rule has been tried in both Argentina and Brazil.

Kohli is also interested in finding out whether or not democratic or non-democratic regimes fare better economically. He compares the experiences of five rather democratic countries with five authoritarian countries and concludes:

1. Democratic regimes as LDCs have been able to generate reasonable rates of economic growth and are thus are not inimical to systems of governance in LDCs.
2. Authoritarian regimes are more likely to enjoy periods of "hyper-growth".
3. Income inequality is often exacerbated under authoritarian rule whereas under democratic rule income inequality declines.
4. Authoritarian regimes are more likely to borrow extensively abroad, which Kohli attributes to the easier access such regimes might have since foreign commercial lenders may have more confidence in such regimes to generate requisite growth.

Part of Kohli's explanation for why authoritarian regimes have been able to do a little better in the growth department is based on the idea that such regimes find it easier to mobilize resources through government saving, i.e., they are more willing to tax and not spend revenues on consumption, since they can avoid the politics of interest groups better than can democratic regimes. Such analysis is perhaps consistent with the Harrod-Domar growth model of the closed economy. However, such analysis ignores international flows. The fact that these governments were willing to borrow abroad to sustain growth during difficult periods may have had more to do with their being able to generate higher growth rates than did their ability to mobilize domestic resources.

The Judiciary. As a major institution of the state some consideration of the functioning of the judiciary is warranted, especially in regard to rent-seeking and the enforcement of law related to rents.

Tullock (1984) sees the jury system, basing its decisions upon the senses of morality and fairness rather than following the letter of the law, as inimical to rent-seeking. Once a monopoly is granted by government the jury system may not cooperate in its enforcement. A jury might reduce the value of rents sought since their enforcement cannot be relied upon. To the extent that trial judges are independent and professionals of the court they are more likely to interpret the law strictly and to enforce rents, thus making rents more certain and valuable.

Landes and Posner (1974) discuss the role of the independent judiciary. Essentially, their conclusion is that an independent judiciary can be better counted upon to enforce the laws of a past legislature than one that is dependent upon the current legislature. Their analysis, however, is based upon the situation in U.S. politics, and it assumes that legislatures are shorter lived than supreme courts. The situation in most African countries (and the Third World, in general) may be quite different. Where most decision making is within the executive branch and courts are subservient to the executive branch the staying power is usually greater among the executives than among the jurors. Thus, the longevity of the regime, at least those regimes where executive power is strongest, may very well exceed the longevity of the court, in which case rent-seekers might have greater surety of having legislation enforced as designed.

The New Political Economy. The new political economy largely postulates a framework of political institutions and behavior as found in industrialized, western countries. The state is usually seen as passive and the focus is on the activities of interest groups to get legislation favorable to themselves passed by politicians (within the framework of political parties facing opposition) whose main concern is self-interest, especially in terms of electoral success. Yet, for Africa, the framework appears at first brush to be irrelevant. African countries generally do not encompass multiparty systems and the role of the state in the affairs of the economy has usually been seen as anything but passive.

Findlay (1989) asks if the "New Political Economy" is relevant in the Third World. Findlay's answer is affirmative. He extends the idea of the autonomous state as applied to conditions prevailing in a number of developing countries. Findlay, concerned with the extraction of surplus by the autonomous state, applies his model to Turkey (which he describes as having moved from a surplus-maximizing to a developmental dictatorship), India ("a successor state to a gunpowder empire"), Africa (mentioning, particularly, the role of marketing boards), Latin America (with diverse polities moving through oligarchy to populism to bureaucratic-authoritarianism) and the Tigers of East Asia (Hong Kong, Korea, Singapore and Taiwan). While Findlay's attitude is positive and his approach somewhat refreshing, the approach is almost too general. We can almost classify every country into its own category or type. Also, the "surplus extraction," while apparent in the surpluses extracted by Africa's agricultural boards, is nonetheless very unclear and probably not empirically visible.

Ashoff (1988) discusses the relevance of rent-seeking theory to developing countries. To the extent that rent-seeking theory argues for the case of "mehr Markt" (i.e., more market) two questions of applicability remain: (1) What is the origin of the "competent" state that arises in some positive cases? (2) What are the recommendations for countries where state and bureaucratic capacity are nearly non-existent, more market?

The first question, in particular, goes right to the point. If rent-seeking theory implies little more than "mehr Markt" then as far as providing policy implications for development it goes little beyond shouting "get the prices right."[31]

Ashoff concludes that the rent-seeking approach is not very useful in providing guidance for development policy since it ignores the severe distortions and market imperfections existent in developing countries and ignores the historical function of the state in those countries. Additionally, as summed in his two questions above, Ashoff feels the approach has little relevance for developing countries since its predetermined answer for policy is the elimination of the state's activities that impinge on the market.

Ashoff's difficulty in seeing the relevance of rent-seeking theory to development may simply arise from the fact that there had been, until the time of this writing, very little attempt to directly apply the approach to developing countries. Simply complaining about the foregone conclusions that seem to be generated by some economists who have been concerned with rent-seeking theory is inadequate. Ashoff made no real attempt to apply the theory himself.

Grindle (1989) criticizes the proponents of the "New Political Economy" stating that their theory of the state is based on the experiences with society-centric models, especially that of the United States. Instead, political economists seeking to understand the role of the state in the development process need to better investigate the dynamics of policy making and implementation in developing countries. She sums up her criticism of the approach, "Development economists might begin to feel less beleaguered by what they see as the inevitable hegemony of politically rational behavior over the collective economic good if they believed more fully in the possibility that political values -- the compromise of conflicting interests, the search for more equitable solutions to public problems, the achievement of social and political stability based on a reasonable set of rules about how collective problems are best resolved, the creation of public trust based on a shared sense of legitimate authority, ... all have value equal to the achievement of economic efficiency."

Grindle is correct to point out that things other than economic efficiency have importance. I do not believe, however, that this has been disputed. The importance of what Grindle brings out is probably not what she seems to indicate are her most important points, instead, the need to understand the process and goals of policy making in developing countries is crucial to understanding the role of government in development. This, however, can best be investigated beginning with analysis of the institutional and incentive arrangements prevailing in particular countries. It is true that non-economic goals may be the initial reasons for certain policies (such as those of African Socialism), but, the persistence of such policies in the face of their obvious failings (which have been well documented) demands answers in terms of who benefits from "bad" policy and how do these beneficiaries maintain such policies when they obviously are detrimental to the many.

Summary. This review indicates the state of confusion regarding the role of the state in the development process. The latest contributions to this literature are sometimes referred to as the "New Political Economy." The new political economy essentially attributes similar rational behavior to state institutions, politicians and bureaucrats as has generally been attributed to firms, households and individuals. This is a radical departure from the traditional view among economists that the state functioned to maximize national welfare. It is also quite distinct from Marxists who see the state as the instrument of one class against others.

Conclusions

Keynesian models of economic growth have stressed the importance of investment. Keynesian models do not emphasize full employment of factors. Indeed, full employment occurs either by chance or as the result of government policies. Investment, the most important determinant of growth, is not driven by maximizing behavior of economic agents. To the extent that investment is 'inadequate' Keynesian theories generally assume that public policy and public investment can increase investment and the rate of growth. There is no assumption of diminishing returns to factors, no substitution among factors, and no theoretical limit to growth.

Neo-classical models assume returns-maximizing behavior by laborers and capitalists. Such behavior is rational and, unlike Keynesian models, tends toward stable, full employment. All factors are used for productive purposes and with the highest returns and lowest costs that are technically feasible, consistent with standard production function theories. While Keynesian models generate all growth from investment, neo-classical models generate growth from both investment and labor growth. Diminishing returns to factors ensure that a steady state will one day be attained and without technological progress growth in per capita (laborer) output cannot continue indefinitely.

The most remarkable aspect of the production function approach to economic growth that has dominated the literature is that up to 80 percent of long-run growth has been attributed to technological progress with actual measures of technological progress seldom being included in empirical models. Some models have attempted to incorporate technological growth by including factors that might be expected to affect the rate of technological progress. Improvements in understanding and modeling technological progress have come about in recent endogenous growth models.

The present state of play in growth theory revolves around increasing returns to capital, technological progress and endogenous models of investment, population growth and growth in knowledge. My research cannot be seen as the next logical step in this progression. Growth modeling has concentrated on long-run trends. I seek to explain trends in the medium term. Since technological progress, investment and savings proclivities and population growth seem to reflect long-term trends and are sometimes treated as endogenously determined in some growth models (such as Barro's and Romer's) they can probably be treated as exogenous factors in empirical models that seek to explain growth in the shorter- to medium-term. More important, however, is my contention that growth theories have handled resource use efficiency inefficiently and have accorded very little role to the nature of the state. Rent-seeking theories help explain why resources are not productively used, yet rent-seeking theorists have provided almost zero contribution to our understanding of growth.[32]

Finally, rent-seeking theories have been entirely too abstract. While the rent-seeking and public choice theorists have been chanting that institutions matter they have relied upon metaphors such as lotteries and negotiations between Friday and Crusoe and have not addressed themselves to the real life institutional and constitutional arrangements.

An important test of a theory is to see how well it explains reality. Neo-classical growth models imply that poorer countries will grow faster than richer. Yet, Africa, the poorest continent, has been experiencing the slowest growth, with the rich countries of the North experiencing much more rapid growth over the past three decades. Neo-classical models cannot account for declines in per worker output, yet per capita income and per worker output have been declining in much of Africa for the past decade and a half. Neo-classical theory predicts the movement of capital from the capital abundant countries of the North to the labor abundant of the South. Yet capital flows to Africa have been trickles, and on a net basis have been outflows for several countries. Clearly, neo-classical growth theories in their present state do little to explain Africa's dismal economic performance since independence.

In many ways the neo-classical growth theories have improved considerably upon the Keynesian theories. The most important improvement has been the assumption of rational behavior. The neo-classical models assume that rational behavior causes economic agents to choose between the most productive activities. I posit that, instead, economic agents choose between those activities yielding the highest private returns and that these are not always productive activities.

Notes

1. See Recent Trends in Developing Countries, by the World Bank (1989).
2. Schumpeter makes the exact same recommendation.
3. For an extensive survey of neoclassical growth models, and especially discussions of long-run convergence models, see Britto (1973).
4. That is, the warranted rate, which in this case is the rate of growth in output and capital, grows at the natural rate, or the rate of growth of the labor force.
5. Hahn and Mathews (1965, pp. 34-43) provide a concise and thorough survey of the two sector models, as well as mathematical growth models in general. Johnson (1971) also provides an excellent discussion of two-sector models of growth.
6. See Denison (1974) page 149.
7. See the next section and the discussion of the Romer model.
8. This is also quoted in Anderson (1987).
9. I discuss this point further in the Appendix.
10. These were not the first economists to posit that technological advances were endogenously caused. Although David Ricardo and almost all the classical and neo-classical economists assumed technological progress fell from heaven Adam Smith in the Wealth of Nations regarded technological progress as the result of the innovation of capitalist rationality, especially as resulting from an expansion of the market and the division of labor such expansion allows. Smith felt that technical progress, or advancing in the "fund of knowledge" was related to the stock (i.e., capital stock). (See Adelman 1961: Chap. 2) Even Karl Marx saw technological progress as a result of cutthroat competition among capitalists, although he also saw the same competition eventually reduce the rate of profits to zero. Denison (1961, 1985) obviously saw increasing returns and technological improvements as quantifiable components of growth, with a much de-emphasized attribution to investment.
11. For time series analysis it may be easy to indicate this effect. However, in cross-country analysis it would be difficult to distinguish between the size of the capital stock and the size of the market. Thus, economies of scale and the build-up in knowledge associated with the size of capital stock would be indistinguishable.

12. For a survey of the theory and evidence related to growth see Easterly and Wetzel (1989). This section of the paper draws heavily from that source.

13. See Easterly (1989), Barro (1989), Gemmel (1983), Grossman (1988), Knight and Sabot (1988), and Landau (1986). Many precursors are referenced in these articles.

14. See the discussion in the Appendix.

15. Actually, Easterly refers to these expenditures as "saving."

16. The negative effects of taxation were derived as distortion on types of capital and discussed earlier.

17. See particularly World Bank (1989a) for details of the literature.

18. Included in Barro (1989), Kormendi and Meguire (1985).

19. See Gallagher (1989) for a breakdown in economic growth rates for the developing countries for the period 1975-1988.

20. When income growth is the dependent variable and when including these two dummy variables the R^2 = .56, but if we drop these two dummies, the R^2 only comes to .45.

21. My emphasis.

22. See Bhagwati's Table 1.

23. More than two were actually investigated.

24. In the Tullock version the optimal r, which represents the probability of gaining the rent in the lottery process, r equals $N/(N-1)$. In the limit (i.e., $N \rightarrow \infty$) the entire rent will be dissipated and this term reduces to W/N.

25. While rents give incentive to overthrow the state they also provide great incentive to maintain the state by those in power. Rents also provide those in power with greater resources to maintain their power, thus there seems to be an identification problem in their specification. Also, Mbaku and Paul use positive trade balances as indication of rents generated from trade intervention. There are many better indicators than this, such as the amount of tariff revenues, or World Bank (1987) indicators of trade orientation. The entire analysis suffers from such sloppy application.

26. We will see how in the next two chapters my own extended theory of rent-seeking both agrees that interest group behavior can be expected to lower growth rates and disagrees with Olson when he says that "The efficiency of an economy may be increased either by making narrow special-interest groups weaker or by making the government stronger in relation to them."

27. Tullock's proposition is discussed in more detail in Chapter 3.

28. Weak diminishing returns to scale are exhibited in sectors where the size of the market increases the winner take all prize that is earned by "super stars." For instance, Bill Cosby could only earn $93 million a year in the US entertainment industry. He would not make nearly that much if he were in the television industry in Germany. In the same vein, the top ping pong champion in the world, though he have equal ability, will not earn anywhere near what the top US basketball star will make. The "winner take all" aspect of "super star" economics associates the top returns to super stars with the size of the market they face.

29. See P. Bardhan (1988).

30. See Kohli (1986).

31. "Getting the prices right" need not imply free markets. For instance, the IMF has been suggesting getting the exchange rate "right" long before it started talking about implementing free trades in currency. Additionally, where market prices would not reflect real externalities, getting the prices right may quite clearly be a call for more, not less, intervention.

32. Except, of course, for the recent contribution by Murphy et al.

3

Rent-Seeking Theory and African Regimes

Drawing on concepts of rent-seeking found in Tullock (1967 and 1984) and Krueger (1974) and the broader concept of "directly unproductive profit seeking" (DUP) found in Bhagwati (1982) a broader version of rent-seeking is reached. This broader concept includes not only the traditional waste of resources devoted to attaining rents but also similar instances where resources are devoted to seeking profit or generating government revenues without adding to the flow of goods and services. This broader concept is linked to the theory of competitive rent-seeking. Non-market decision making is also discussed and related to the waste of resources devoted to influencing the distribution of public goods, services and transfers.

African governments are categorized by the degree of political pluralism and the likely degree of competition for rents. Ekelund and Tollison's (1981) hypothesis that rent-seeking becomes more costly to potential rent-seekers when there is greater competition for rents from the rise of democratic institutions is generalized. This generalization leads to a number of hypotheses, which are tested in Chapter 4.

Rent-Seeking

The concept of rent-seeking and related resource waste used in this paper focuses on actions that seek to alter, enforce, maintain or circumvent government policies which entail transfers of income. Certain policy caused distortions create opportunities for or are the result of rent-seeking activities. These activities may entail direct waste of resources (such as over-investment in industrial capacity to qualify for import licenses) or transfers (such as bribes). Some of these are presented in the following table.

Table 3.1:   Rent Opportunities

Opportunity	Activity	Waste/Transfer
1. Tariffs	- Lobbying	both
	- Enforcement	waste
	- Smuggling	both
	- Misallocation	waste
2. Domestic Monopoly	- Lobbying	both
	- Enforcement	waste
	- Cheating	both
	- Misallocation	waste
3. Credit Rationing	- Lobbying	both
	- Enforcement	waste
	- Black Market	waste
	- Misallocation	waste
4. Foreign Exchange Rationing	- Lobbying	both
	- Capital Flight	waste
	- Misallocation	waste
5. Government Allocation	- Lobbying	both
	- Misallocation	waste
6. Domestic Monopsony (e.g., agricultural marketing boards)	- Misallocation	waste
	- Smuggling	both

In each case there is the traditional misallocation of resources. For instance, under-valued foreign exchange rationed by the central bank favors production processes that rely on imported inputs, especially foreign produced capital goods. High tariffs encourage the production of import substitutes, the domestic resource cost of which generally exceed their domestic value, waste domestic resources and foreign exchange. Rationing of credit at low or negative real rates of interest over-encourages capital intensive investment, and may allocate credit to the not optimally productive industries or firms. Smuggling wastes the resources used to circumvent customs. Bribes are transfers from rent-seekers to officials, such as legislators, regulators or enforcement agents. As transfers these funds do not immediately entail the direct waste of resources.[1] They do, however, raise the cost of doing business. Also, such transfers may often leave the country as "hot money" and in this way reduce the accumulation of capital for reinvestment within the country. Black market exchange of currencies entails similar costs of enforcement and evading the law. Sometimes allocations of foreign exchange are tied to plant capacity,[2] which prompts over-investment in facilities. Stereotypically, government misallocates resources and mixes resources inefficiently.[3]

Rents are harvested in many ways. For instance, the state may sell monopoly rights. The monopolist is then free to extract rents by selling his product in a protected market at a price higher than marginal cost. Sometimes rents are harvested directly by governments, especially through the operation of public enterprises or agricultural marketing boards. At other times, rents are harvested by politicians, usually, but not always, in partnership with others. For instance, rent-seeking activities, such as lobbying, can influence politicians to grant a monopoly for the "national good." Or, a politician may grant himself a monopoly, grant a monopoly to his family or cronies, or sell a monopoly to a third party for a bribe.

Other politicians may seek rents without the creation of an apparent monopoly. Red tape and the power officials have to waste private individuals' time and energy forms a basis for rent harvesting, a transfer of income from the beleaguered private businessman to the government official.

When public revenues are short and government's ability to meet its financial obligations are rationed the opportunity for those government officials empowered with deciding who gets paid how much and when increases. For instance, during the 1980s government arrears to domestic vendors in Liberia often exceeded $70 million. Payment of part of those arrears naturally gives opportunity for side payments to specific government officials. Such side payments, along with the delays and uncertainties of getting payment for completed work, drive up the cost of doing business with the government, costs which are incorporated in contracts and passed on to the general public.

Patronage employment[4] may represent a waste of public resources for the gains of politicians or the state and create a vested interest group, public employees. Patronage, in the form of jobs, is often used to gain political support.[5] Often jobs are given to members of a particular ethnic group, such as the Krahn in Liberia under Doe, or the Kikuyu under British rule in Kenya. In Africa, however, patronage is often an attempt to buy urban peace. Government employees become a group with which to reckon. Their attempts to save their positions in the face of austerity have been quite successful, as casual inspection of government budgets reveals.[6]

Enforcing Rents

Enforcement is an integral part of rent-seeking. Unless rents can be enforced, rent-seeking can have no payoff. For instance, an unenforced tariff offers no protection to domestic would-be import-substituting producers (nor does it generate government revenues), since illegal imports could drive the domestic price of the dutiable commodity to the world price level. Enforcement of monopoly rights is necessary or a monopoly does not exist.

Enforcement is often the duty of the bureau of customs, bureau of excise (often regulates output), the police and the courts. Enforcement offers opportunities to seek rents to the enforcement agents. For instance, customs agents can be bribed. While such bribery allows imports to come into the country without paying the tariff the enforcement, in the form of a bribe, still implies a cost to the smuggler. In general, the more effort the state puts into enforcement of rents the more costly it is to try to circumvent regulation, tariffs, or taxes and the more valuable the initial rent. Since enforcement raises the value of rents generated by government policies it makes sense that governments will devote resources to enforcement.

Non-Market Decision Making

Non-market decision making takes place in many institutional settings: in families, local cooperatives, and corporations, to name just a few. Some of these institutional settings involve voting, such as cooperatives, whereas others operate based upon hierarchical lines of authority, such as the family or the corporation. Continued participation in cooperatives, corporations and, to a lesser extent, families, is voluntary. One is bound to the institutional decisions only through free association. If allocation by the institution is considered by a member to be unfavorable the member can disassociate himself. To the extent he maintains his association even when allocations are not seen as being in the member's favor we must assume some externality exists to entice the member to maintain association.

Non-market allocation of resources through government is significantly different from free associations. Dissatisfaction with the allocation process of government cannot easily be expressed through termination of association. Citizens can forfeit their association with the rules, regulations and governance of government, but usually at very high cost; such costs might include leaving one's homeland and family, organizing and carrying out coup d'etat, or seeking to reform the process from within. Each of these costs is sufficiently high to differentiate association with government from participation in other types of institutions.[7] Because government subjugation or participation is not by free association, worthwhile externalities cannot be assumed when allocation seems inferior.

Government affects the allocation of resources in two ways: through direct resource allocation in the provision of public services, and through regulation or other market interventions. Direct allocation of public resources depends very much on the dispersion of power and influence. In democracies, allocation may not maximize social welfare, since representatives strive to maintain their political offices, and this depends on how their articulate constituents perceive their performance in office. Positive political performance may have very little to do with Pareto-optimal resource allocation and much more to do with gaining benefits for constituencies. Politicians in democratic countries often seek huge amounts of money to maintain their almost constant campaign efforts. This may make them susceptible to the influence of lobbyists with narrow interests, as might their own greed. Politicians may decide to trade off some high ideals in order to gain the wherewithal that will enable them to continue the struggle into the next legislature, or to lead a better life.

Willingness to Rent-Seek

There are essentially three types of costs the rent-seeker faces. The first refers to the wasted resources devoted directly toward the rent-seeking activity. These include the resources (say, capital and labor) devoted to circumventing law, investing in facilities and activities for the legitimate purposes of seeking to have law changed (e.g., lobbying) or the status quo protected, or investing in facilities that are uneconomic but necessary to gain capital or foreign exchange allocations.[8] These costs are direct and are borne in the first round of incidence by the rent-seeker, and represent a true waste of resources.

Direct costs are the usual costs that one expects to consider when investigating the waste of resources of rent-seeking. The amount of resources that would have to be wasted in unproductive activities in order for the rent-seeker to attain income will vary according to the institutional structure of the country,[9] some geographical features of the country (say, in the case of smuggling) and the amount of resources available for enforcement.

The second set of costs can be referred to as administrative. Such costs refer to the costs of administering code or law. These may include tax expenditures that arise from incentives granted foreign investors, which represent a transfer rather than the actual waste of the country's resources. Code enforcement, such as the labor expended on enforcing tariffs and production quotas (salaries of the Customs and Excise bureaus) represents a waste of resources but also raises the costs facing the rent-seeker. In the first round of incidence these costs are borne by the treasury and the public in general, but also raise the costs facing the rent-seeker.

The third set of costs facing the rent-seeker are transfers. These may be illicit. They need not, in and of themselves, lead to the direct waste of society's resources. These costs include bribes to government officials, politicians, enforcement agents and the like. However, they may also include royalties paid for the extraction of natural resources.

Other transfers may include the social requirements mandated in concession agreements, where enclave extractive (mining or forestry, for instance) industries are required to provide housing, medical and schooling benefits for their employees, and wages, above and beyond the economic value of the labor provided. Such transfers need not reduce output, but in that they raise the cost of doing business they may reduce incentives to invest. The first round of incidence falls on the rent-seeker.

In the case of illicit transfers, such as bribes to politicians, the resources available for domestic production may be reduced through capital flight. That is, when politicians take bribes it can be expected that a goodly part of the illicit receipts will leave the country. The most basic, in the sense that they are common in all countries, of these costs have to do with administration and enforcement; protecting borders, regulating production, allocating foreign exchange and subsidized investment funds, etc. The costs of enforcing rents, or protecting one's assets and income from rent-seekers, are the most basic costs. These costs, in the abstract, are unrelated to the type of institutional arrangements in society and are identical under absolute monarchy and pure democracy, or at least across countries we should expect a constant cost of rent-seeking regardless of institutional arrangements.

Institutional costs are related to the degree of power centralization of the state. Ekelund and Tollison take this point of view.

> When the locus of power to rent-seek shifted from the monarch (in England) to Parliament via more stringent controls on the King, the cost of supplying regulation through legislative enactment rose, for reasons suggested by the theory of public choice. Lobbying costs and non-durability of laws passed due to competition within the judiciary contributed to the decline of mercantilism in England.   (Ekelund and Tollison 1981: 149)

Institutional costs entail those costs of lobbying, bribery, and uncertainty (including resources devoted to raising certainty) associated with rent-seeking. In the case of the absolute monarch, there is no institution related uncertainty nor are there lobbying costs when it is the monarch himself who is the rent-seeker. The monarch does not have to share his rent nor, if he is an absolute monarch, does he have to worry about the uncertainty of the legislative or judicial branches undermining him. In contrast, under a democratic system of great institutional competition, where the legislative and executive branches of government must both be lobbied and influenced, where public opinion and public accountability must be factored into decisions, and where the certainty of judicial enforcement is in question, institutional costs will be great. Rent-seekers' utility of income from rents is reduced when these rents are at risk of being overturned by any branch of government. Additionally, the costs of influence reduce the net return to the rent-seeker.

In general, economic agents should be indifferent to the source of their returns. That is, an opportunity to earn profit from productive use of resources or to garner a similar return from non-productive uses of resources should weigh equally in an income maximizing utility function, other things equal. Thus, we can look at rent-seeking within the context that such activity merely represents an alternative source of income.

Assuming income maximizing behavior, people are willing to rent-seek up to the point where the net marginal return to rent- seeking equals the marginal return to using their resources in productive ways.[10] An absolute monarch will equate the marginal costs of rent-seeking to the cost of enforcing his rent. In turn, the marginal return to rent-seeking will be equated to the marginal return to productive use of resources. Under democratic forms of the state marginal rents, net of institutional costs, will be equated to the marginal return from using the same resources in productive pursuits. Figure 3.1 illustrates the willingness to rent-seek in two societies. Under absolute monarchy the return maximizing amount of rent-seeking is indicated by RA, which is where the cost of rent enforcement equals the expected marginal rent attained, which is also equal to the marginal return that could have been expected from productive use of resources.

R*, on the other hand, represents the outcome in a democratic society. At R* marginal returns to rent-seeking net of institutional costs are equated to the marginal returns to the productive use of resources.

C represents the institutional costs, which reduces the rent-seeker's net return. If C is proportional to the marginal return to rent-seeking then net marginal rent can be represented by $MR(1-c)$ -- where $C =$

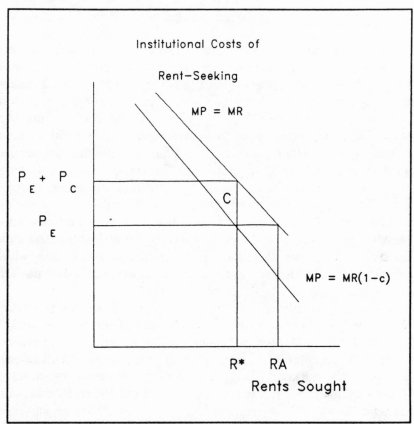

Figure 3.1

cMR -- which will equal marginal return from productive resource use, such that MR(1-c) = MP. Under absolute monarchy the price paid by rent-seekers is P_E, while under the democratic system the price of rents would be $P_E + P_C$.

Ekelund and Tollison illustrated that the rising power of Parliament in England competed with the monarch in the granting of monopolies and thereby hindered the monarch's ability to ensure monopolies. Similarly, we can expect that competing components of government in modern day Africa will raise the costs facing rent-seekers.

Political Regimes

The role of institutions and the constitutional setting are integral
to this analysis. For instance, Tullock (1984) sees the dependence on
the jury system for settling disputes as raising the cost of rent-seeking
to such high levels that those countries which have a strong,
functioning jury system will likely suffer less from rent-seeking. His
reasoning is that juries often tend to disregard the letter of the law,
especially when they fail to see the need for such laws or if they feel
a law is morally invalid. In terms of enforcement, jury systems make
enforcement of rents less certain. To the extent enforcement of rights
and rents is less certain rent-seeking is less attractive.

The growth in the number of institutions that must be lobbied and
relied upon to provide and enforce rents must both increase the direct
costs potential rent-seekers face as well as raise the uncertainty of the
outcome of the efforts and the uncertainty of rent enforcement. This
is consistent with Reid (1977), who mentions that

> ... attempts to capture the coercive power of the state become
> more likely as the relative cost of achieving equivalent results
> within the goods market increases, either because competition in
> the goods market is keener or because competition in the
> political market is relaxed.   (Reid 1977: 309-310)

At first brush it seems that at one extreme where the polity can be
described as pluralistic or democratic there will be relatively little rent-
seeking. At the other extreme, absolute monarchies would experience
the greatest rent-seeking, cet. par. In modern day Africa there are no
absolute monarchies but there are similar regimes, such as
dictatorships. Other regimes that approach this lack of effective
institutional competition include regimes run by military juntas or by
strong one party systems.

Various categorizations of the types of government have been used
in analyses of the relationship between the state and the economy.
Findlay (1989), Kohli (1986), Grindle (1989) and others have all
considered the relationship between the state and the economy but
none of their classifications have approached the problem of
categorizing an array of countries by the degree of rent-competition
among their institutions. Ekelund and Tollison, of course, have

provided a key, but they only compared two countries. A more comprehensive categorization is in order.

Chazan, Mortimer, and Rothchild (1988) provide a set of categories which they apply to Africa. These include: pluralistic, administrative-hegemonical, party-mobilizing, party-centrist, personal-coercive, populist, and ambiguous regimes. In pluralistic regimes, such as Botswana and Mauritius, there is competition among political parties with fairly vibrant representative systems. There is separation of powers with the legislative, executive and the judicial systems all keeping watch on each other. There is also likely to be considerable competition, although less so, in regimes fitting the administrative-hegemonical description. Administrative-hegemonical, such as Kenya under Kenyatta and perhaps less so under Moi, regimes have three key institutions: the executive, the administrative and the enforcement[11] apparatus. Main policy decision-making is centralized around the leader and his close advisers. Specific technical and professional decision-making is carried out in the bureaucracy. The military's role is mainly for national defense and is well restrained. The bureaucratic and judicial systems maintain a degree of autonomy vis-a-vis each other but both are less than fully autonomous from the executive. These regimes pay considerable attention to the need for balancing various interests, especially ethnic groups, and they seek to maintain a degree of pluralism.

The other regime types either exhibit less institutional competition or they are too uncertain to categorize in this manner. For instance, the populist regimes usually arose in response to somewhat dictatorial but untenable regimes. These regimes have usually been transitional, not being seen as having taken hold. At the same time, they have usually been reformist and have in some instances sought to disperse power (Rawlings in Ghana, e.g.), have maintained fairly centralized power structures (Sankara in Burkina Faso, Doe during the beginning of his rule in Liberia, e.g.). Party-mobilizing (Ghana under Nkrumah, or Guinea under Sekou Toure, e.g.) and party-centrist regimes (Angola under dos Santos, or Ethiopia under Mengistu, e.g.) centralize power around the leader and the party, or the party and the party's ideals. The countries categorized as ambiguous are just that. Uganda under Amin, Central African Republic (or Empire) under Bokassa, and possibly the later years of Doe's rule in Liberia, are examples of the personal-coercive regime. Under these regimes strong leaders (in terms of ruthlessness and power) maintain strict control over the military and the police, while the bureaucracy, political machinery and judicial system are all subject to the whims of the ruler, the commander in chief. Uganda in the 1980s, Chad and the Sudan throughout most of the 1980s have been countries where institutional settings have been too fluid to classify, but the degree of general uncertainty approaches anarchy, leading to rent-seeking based on short term extraction of rents by force with little concern for the future.[12]

While the discussion helps illuminate the relationship between regime type and competition for rents, Chazan et al. (1988) do not provide information for every African country and their classification does not readily lend itself to quantitative analysis. Gastil (1987)[13] provides two indices of rights (political and personal/economic) for the periods 1973, 1975-86. In Gastil's index the higher the number the lower the degree of rights. The lowest numbers were reserved for those countries where political and personal rights were most secure. Gastil's index is based on surveys taken in 1973, and annually from 1975 to 1986, with annual rankings available. The survey included a number of factors, namely: electoral process of electing chief authority, election of legislature, fairness of election laws in reflecting voter preferences, multiple or single party systems, significance of opposition vote, degree of military interference, denial of political rights to major groups, centralization of political power, and de facto opposition power (how much consensus building there is in the political process).

Civil liberty rankings work much the same as political freedom rankings and there is a high correlation between the two. States that guarantee political freedom generally also guarantee civil rights. And, where political oppression is the norm few people enjoy civil rights. The civil liberties survey check list includes: freedom of the news media, open public discussion, freedom of assembly and demonstration, independent judiciary and security forces, freedom from officially sanctioned violence, freedom to organize trade unions or other economic cooperative organizations, freedom of religion, personal rights (including property, travel and choice of residence), freedom from economic dependency (such as on landlords -- freedom from oligarchies or latifundistas) and freedom from "gross socioeconomic inequality," and freedom from "gross government indifference" or corruption.

Countries are ranked by political and civil freedom[14] from 1 (greatest freedom) to 7 (least freedom). These are comparative rankings rather than absolute. For political rights, states ranked (1) have a fully competitive electoral process and those elected actually rule. Most Western European countries, Canada and the U.S. are ranked (1). No African countries are ranked (1). Countries ranked (2) enjoy a working electoral process but exhibit other factors, such as extreme economic inequality, illiteracy, or intimidating violence, which effectively tend to reduce political competition. In Africa, only Botswana and Mauritius are ranked (2). Rankings (3) to (5) indicate progressively less democratic systems of government. States ranked (6) do not have elections and are ruled by a dictator or a small group or junta. But, the rulers are usually constrained in some ways, say by Islamic law or by the threat of public revolt. Most countries in Africa are ranked either (6) or (7). (7) is despotic, and includes one-third of African countries. Civil freedom rankings are very similar.

These political and personal freedom index numbers were averaged for each country for the respective periods (1975-81 and 1981-86), then inverted and multiplied by 100. This manipulation then reserves the highest scores for the countries with the greatest freedoms. For instance, in Table 3.2 in 1981-86 Mauritius, scoring the highest of the group, enjoyed the highest degree of rights, followed closely by Botswana and the Gambia. Angola, Benin, Central African Republic, Mozambique and Somalia were among the poorest ranked, although there were several other countries that fall into the same category. It is heartening to note the partial restoration of rights in Uganda (and somewhat in Central Africa) in the 1980s. Unfortunately, more countries seem to exhibit deterioration in rights compared to those few countries where rights have been on the upswing. The purpose of this manipulation is solely to generate an indicator that rises with freedoms as opposed to Gastil's index which declines with freedoms. This manipulation does not alter the meaning of the index nor does it alter the statistical properties of the index. For a more in-depth discussion of the variety of indicators that were reviewed and why the Gastil index was selected see the Appendix.

Table 3.2: Degree of Political Pluralism:

	1975-81	1981-86
Angola	8	7
Benin	7	7
Botswana	20	20
Burkina Faso	12	8
Burundi	8	8
Cameroon	9	8
Central Afr. Rep.	7	8
Chad	8	8
Comoros	13	10
Congo	8	8
Cote d' Ivoire	9	9
Djibouti	16	11
Equatorial Guinea	8	8
Ethiopia	8	7
Gabon	8	8
Gambia	25	17
Ghana	10	10
Guinea	7	8
Guinea-Bissau	8	8
Kenya	10	10
Lesotho	11	10
Liberia	10	9
Madagascar	9	9
Malawi	8	8
Mali	7	8
Mauritania	8	8
Mauritius	20	22
Mozambique	7	8
Niger	8	8
Nigeria	12	12
Rwanda	8	8
Sao Tome & Principe	9	8
Senegal	11	13
Seychelles	13	8
Sierra Leone	10	10
Somalia	7	7
Sudan	9	9

Continued... Table 3.2: Degree of Political Pluralism:

	1975-81	1981-86
Swaziland	10	10
Tanzania	8	8
Togo	8	8
Uganda	8	11
Zaire	8	8
Zambia	10	8
Zimbabwe	10	11

These values are by no means precise. Nonetheless, this scoring
hints to at least one interesting partial result; an apparent relationship

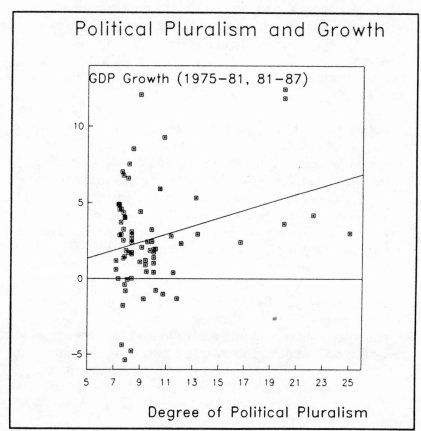

Figure 3.2

between the degree of institutional competition for rents and economic growth across countries. Figure 3.2 is a scatter plot of economic growth rates and the degree of institutional competition for rents for 28 African countries during the periods 1975-81 and 1981-87. While this scatter plot (and the regression generated trend line) indicate some positive relationship between political pluralism and economic growth the statistical relationship is dominated by extreme cases (outliers) and is not conclusive, in and of itself.

Rent-Seeking and Growth

The types of costs rent-seeking imposes on an economy have been presented in Table 3.1. These costs have a dynamic aspect, i.e., that rent-seeking retards growth. These costs quite obviously lower the level of resources available for productive purposes in a country but a dynamic theory is necessary to determine the impact on growth.

According to Tullock (1984) "static inefficiencies" (such as the opportunities in Table III.1) do not cause slower growth, per se, but cause growth from a lower basis. For example

Let us consider the condition of the society in which these traditional economic inefficiencies exist but in which there is no rent-seeking, i.e., no resources are put into attempting to achieve government-granted monopoly, to change regulations in your favor, or to protect yourself against these activities. The first to be said is that there would be a very considerable waste but there would be no dynamic waste in the sense of resources invested in attempting to make society less efficient for private gain.

Everyone would be adjusting optimally to a particular environment. There might be a prohibitive tariff on the import of automobiles and one guild might have a complete monopoly on the manufacture of ball bearings for automobiles, but these would be very much the same as if natural barriers such as expensive raw materials or backward technology were causing difficulty. Human energy would be

> devoted solely and specifically to efficient production subject
> to these hazards.   (Tullock 1984: 225-6)

Tullock cites the case of the early rapid growth of the American colonies, where he claims the highly regulated economy experienced growth but from a low level. "What happens, in essence, is that growth comes from a lower base but it can be quite rapid." (Tullock 1984: 227) Tullock makes the point, however, that this is no reason for not eliminating such inefficiencies. Their elimination would give a spurt of additional growth.

Costs to society of avoiding regulation and taking advantage of static inefficiencies must also be taken into account. The resources wasted on smuggling, bribery of officials, mismanagement of public funds, and legislation related costs tied to monopoly maintenance and enforcement all increase with economic growth. That these costs remain as a constant share of all costs as an economy grows remains to be determined.

<u>Comparative Statics and Exogenous Price Changes.</u> Under what conditions do "static inefficiencies" slow/not slow economic growth? Two opposing cases can be made. The first supporting the view that "static inefficiencies" do not cause slower growth but merely cause growth from a lower level. The second, that proposed by this author, sees "static inefficiencies" as opportunities to rent-seek and slowing growth.[15]

The first supports Tullock's view: Compare two economies with identical endowments. Because of a distortion or "static inefficiency" the second economy only uses part of its resources for productive purposes. The rest of the country's resources can be seen as having been wasted through misallocation. Both economies export all they produce and import all they consume, and are price takers in imports and exports. Both economies export the same product, there is only one factor of production and the factor is fully employed, although in the second country, not fully productive.

Under these circumstances the two economies can be modeled:

$$Y_1 = kXP \tag{3.1}$$

$$Y_2 = k(X-a)P \tag{3.2}$$

where

Y_i is national income in economy i,

P   is the price of the export product,

X   is total resource endowment,

a   is the amount of wasted resources that takes place because of misallocation due to "static inefficiency, and

k   is the technological coefficient, so kX is total exports from country 1, while k(X-a) is the total exports from country 2.

The rate of growth due to an improvement in the international terms of trade for each country can be expressed as

$$(\partial Y/\partial P)/Y$$

Therefore,

$$(\partial Y_1/\partial P) = kX, \text{ and} \tag{3.3}$$

$$(\partial Y_1/\partial P)/Y_1 = kX/Y_1 = kX/kXP = 1/P \tag{3.4}$$

and

$$(\partial Y_2/\partial P)/Y_2 = k(X-a)/Y_2 = k(X-a)/k(X-a)P = 1/P. \tag{3.5}$$

Although country 2 starts off poorer and remains poorer than country 1, the rate of growth for both countries is identical.

In the second case, when "static inefficiencies" are as opportunities to rent-seek, the waste of resources (a) increases when income rises. Thus, the case is modified when (a) is seen as being positively related to the level of income, i.e., $\partial a/\partial Y > 0$.

For simplicity sake, assume a = cY, where c>0. Then (iii.2) can be rewritten, dropping the subscript for ease:

$$Y_2 = k(X-cY)P \tag{3.6}$$

and   Y = kXP - kcYP

$$Y(1+kcP) = kXP$$

$$Y = kXP/(1+kcP) \tag{3.7}$$

and

$$\frac{\delta Y}{\delta P} = \frac{(1+kcP)(kx)-kXPkc}{(1+kcP)^2}$$

$$= \frac{kX+k^2cPX-k^2XPc}{(1+kcP)^2}$$

and dividing $\partial Y/\partial P$ by Y as expressed in (3.7)

$$\frac{\delta Y/\delta P}{Y} = \frac{kX/(1+kcP)^2}{kXP/(1+kcP)} = \frac{1}{p} \times \frac{1}{1+kcP} < \frac{1}{P}$$

since k, c, P > 0.

Therefore, where "static inefficiencies," in fact, are not "static," and where higher levels of income, spurred by exogenous factors such as an appreciation of the terms of trade, give rise to further opportunities to rent-seek the rate of growth must be slower than in the absence of these opportunities.

By now it should be fairly clear that higher levels of income, resulting from increased external prices (or similar arguments could be made for improvements in productivity), will lead to larger potential rents (higher income would cause a shift in the willingness to rent-seek. However, in a growing economy not only do the opportunities to garner rents increase but so do opportunities to earn income from productive activities.

If policy changes can be ignored, the income elasticities of these sectors of the economy that generate the most rent -- say import-substituting, capital, and foreign exchange markets, as well as the government sector -- lead one to expect that rent opportunities (supply of rents) are also income elastic. For instance, that income elasticity of demand for manufactures (generally a highly protected sector) is high leads one to expect that rents from this sector will grow in proportion to total national product as incomes grow. If "Wagner's Law" holds and government spending is income elastic then we can expect this sector to yield higher rents in proportion to the size of the economy. Additionally, when imports are income elastic then rents from this sector will also rise in proportion to the economy as incomes grow. For the same reasons there will be more rent-seeking, cet. par., where incomes are higher, since manufacturing, trade, government, are all larger shares of the economy in the richer countries. These are hypotheses which will be tested in Chapter 4. For the time being, however, a discussion of "Wagner's Law" is appropriate.

Government Allocation Rises with Incomes. "Wagner's Law" (Wagner, 1890) maintains that public goods are income elastic, i.e., as incomes grow the "demand" for public goods grows even more rapidly.[16]

Table 3.3 presents income (GDP) elasticities of government spending[17] among African countries during the period 1970-87.

Table 3.3: Income Elasticity of Government Spending:

Country	Elasticity	Observations	R-Square
Benin	0.9	8	0.4
Botswana	1.3	16	0.9
Burkina Faso	1.6	15	0.9
Burundi	1.6	14	0.9
Cameroon	1.4	13	0.9
Central Afr.Rep.	-1.3	6	0.5
Comoros	0.1	6	0.1
Cote d' Ivoire	2.3	7	0.6
Ethiopia	3.4	16	0.9
Gambia	0.4	15	0.0
Ghana	1.9	15	0.1
Guinea	-0.6	7	0.0
Guinea-Bissau	0.4	8	0.1
Kenya	1.8	16	0.9
Liberia	3.7	14	0.4
Malawi	1.8	17	0.9
Mauritania	0.4	13	0.0
Mauritius	1.6	15	0.8
Niger	2.0	12	0.7
Nigeria	1.9	16	0.4
Rwanda	2.0	15	0.9

Continuation of Table 3.3:
Income Elasticity of Government Spending in Africa:

Country	Elasticity	Observations	R-Square
Senegal	1.6	13	0.6
Sierra Leone	-0.1	14	0.0
Somalia	1.3	14	0.3
Sudan	1.4	16	0.7
Swaziland	2.3	17	0.8
Tanzania	1.2	16	0.3
Togo	0.2	11	0.0
Uganda	4.4	16	0.8
Zaire	4.0	17	0.7
Zambia	3.3	16	0.3
Zimbabwe	1.7	12	0.8

Sources: World Bank and Author's data files.

In most cases government spending does seem to be elastic in response to increase in GDP. In many of the countries where this has not been so GDP growth has been very uneven may even have declined in absolute terms in more recent years. In these instances factors other than the rate of GDP growth better explain trends in government spending. Among the countries where elasticities are below unity almost all generated R^2s that were very low, indicating that this simple specification is not appropriate in the particular instance.

We can conclude from Table 3.3 that in most instances Government spending in most of Africa has been GDP elastic. Thus, we can expect the ratio of government spending to GDP to rise as GDP rises, therefore related rent-seeking will also rise in share of GDP and a greater proportion of a country's resources will be wasted in rent-seeking activities, thereby slowing economic growth.

Comparative Statics. The rent-seeker is indifferent to the source of gain. The choices the rent-seeker faces are to maximize gain within the constraints of available resources. The objective function is to maximize income, which is gained either from the value of productive output (Q) or from rents (R), thus,

Let $U = Q + R$, where U is the combined total of real goods and services (Q) and rents (R). Since I will assert that resources released from rent-seeking can be used to raise Q, U can be referred to as "potential output." Then assume two sectoral production functions

$$Q = q(K_q, L_q) \text{ and}$$

$$R = r(K_r, K_r)$$

where the subscript $_q$ indicates labor and capital used for productive purposes. The subscript r indicates labor and capital wasted on rent-seeking activities.

If we assume there are only these two sectors and that all resources are fully (but not productively) employed, then the total labor force (L) is equal to the sum of labor used in productive enterprise and the labor wasted in rent-seeking, and likewise for capital, then

$$L = L_q + L_r, \text{ and}$$

$$K = K_q + L_r.$$

Assuming perfectly competitive rent-seeking the marginal products and marginal rents are equalized then the two sector functions can be combined into a single first difference equation

$$\Delta U = \Delta Q + \Delta R = a_0 + a_1(\Delta K_q + \Delta K_r) + a_2(\Delta L_q + \Delta L_r),$$

where a_1 is the marginal product and/or the marginal rent of capital, and a_2 is the marginal product and/or rent of labor.

Of course, we have already established that the degree of rent-competition varies from country to country. In Chapter 4 the model will be extended to include this factor. From this point, however, it is apparent that if rents rise, given the level of resources, this must require a diversion of factors from productive to rent-seeking activity and will reduce Q. Within the context of rising resource availabilities an increase in the share of resources devoted to rent-seeking will slow economic growth, if the share remains the same then growth will be commensurate with the growth in resource availabilities, and, finally, if the share declines economic growth will outpace the increase in resource growth.

Hypotheses

The theory of competitive rent-seeking as discussed above leads to a series of hypotheses warranting empirical testing. The hypotheses are:
1. Where rent-seeking is less costly to the rent-seeker it will be more prevalent. Conversely, where it is more costly there will be less rent-seeking;
2. Rent-seeking is most costly to the rent-seeker where institutional competition for rents is greatest and least costly where institutional competition is at a minimum; and institutional competition for rents is greater where there is more political pluralism.
3. Rent-seeking is income elastic and, equivalently, is more prevalent where per capita incomes are greater.
4. Rent-seeking diverts resources from productive activity and both lowers welfare and slows growth.

Notes

1. But, see Krueger (1974), who explains how bribes to government officials engender waste through the competition for civil service appointments.

2. Bhagwati and Desai (1970) illustrate the allocation of import licenses in LDCs to firms producing certain kinds of goods or which have a minimum of installed industrial capacity.

3. The importance of government direct allocation is further discussed later in this chapter.

4. Reid and Kurth (1988) remind us of Wilson's (1961, p. 370) definition of patronage jobs, "all those posts, distributed at the discretion of political leaders, the pay for which is greater than the value of the public services performed." Other definitions of patronage entail similar uneconomic uses for public employment.

5. Reid and Kurth (1988) discuss patronage, as well as the evolution from patronage through civil service to militant unions. Their major hypothesis is that "public employees are employed optimally by politicians to produce current and future income for politicians." (p. 254) Unless we can equate the maximization of politicians' incomes with the maximization of national welfare it becomes pretty clear that public sector employment often entails less than optimal resource use from a national stand point.

6. Inspection of government budgets in Africa shows that during the 1980s when budgets have contracted allocations have been severely skewed toward personnel costs; with capital spending and spending on maintenance and supplies declining, in some cases, dramatically.

7. Reid (1977) discusses decision making in the "political market." Especially relevant is his discussion of the state and his assertion that "...economic efficiency cannot be presumed to dictate outcomes in the political market." (p. 311)

8. For instance, in some cases foreign exchange allocations are based upon the size of an enterprise's facilities, and capital (investible funds) are sometimes allocated according to industry or industrial capacity.

9. The degree of institutional competition for rents is discussed in the next section.

10. This is rigorously shown in Chapter 4.

11. Chazan et al. refer to the coercive apparatus

12. See Olson (1988).

13. A variety of approaches to ranking, grading and otherwise classifying African regimes is further discussed in the Appendix.

14. See Gastil (1987) pp. 29-39.

15. Olson (1983) makes the case that the behavior of special narrow interest groups stifle innovation and hence they also stifle growth. I do not disagree with Olson's arguments but I feel that technological innovation will not show up as a determinant of growth in the seven year time periods being studied here. I agree that within the framework of rent-seeking we should expect such interest group behavior to have dilatory effects on growth.

16. Ram (1988) tested Wagner's Law with recent data from Summers and Heston (1988) and was unable to confirm it. There are some problems with Ram's testing, however. The first is that he used "government final consumption expenditures" (GFCE) rather than

17. These elasticities are the estimated coefficients the following regression applied to time series data for each country: $\Delta G/G = \alpha_0 + \alpha_1 \Delta Q/Q + \mu$, where G is total government spending and Q is GDP, although in most cases fewer than seventeen observations were actually available. The purpose of this regression is to calculate elasticities and not to indicate causality. The significance of the coefficients therefore would be meaningless.

4

Model and Estimations

The theory of competitive rent-seeking discussed in Chapter 3 yields a number of hypotheses. To investigate these hypotheses I have derived a formal, general model of rent-seeking and a rent-augmented growth model, which posit a number of relationships as well as a number of estimable equations. The model assumes that economic agents are indifferent to the source of income and they allocate resources between productive use and rent-seeking in attempting to maximize returns.

Part A develops the general, rent-augmented growth model. Then a number of estimable equations are extracted from the model. Part B illustrates rent calculation. Part C derives an empirically testable growth model, introducing a number of variables that can affect growth and rent-seeking. All equations to be estimated are marked *. Part D discusses the methods for estimating the rent-augmented model and comparing it to the neo-classical growth model and provides the estimations. Econometric methods are applied to estimate these equations using data for African countries covering two discrete time periods, 1975-81 and 1981-87, with one observation of averaged values over the time period. The data sample is not uniform, varying in size depending upon the variable. Finally, part E interprets and summarizes the empirical findings.

General Model

Classical growth models did not include optimizing behavior by individuals. Neo-classical growth models include optimizing behavior in that economic agents are assumed to maximize returns to factors in the production of goods and services. Neo-classical models assume that all factors are used for productive purposes. If instead resources are used for unproductive as well as productive purposes then the neo-classical models are biased, indicating lower factor productivity than actually achieved.

The extended theory of rent-seeking of Chapter 3 contains the basis for a rent-seeking augmented economic growth model. In the model there are two sectors. In the first sector labor (L) and capital (K) are productively used to produce goods and services which increase national welfare and raise national income (Q). In the second sector labor and capital are wasted on rent-seeking.

Figure 4.1 presents a transformation curve indicating the trade off between productive output and rents. This transformation curve assumes that all resources are used to produce either rents or goods and services. If the total outcome of what factors are utilized for (the combination of rents and goods and services) is represented by U, and R stands for rents and Q for goods and services,[1] then

$$U = Q + R. \tag{4.1}$$

Both Q and R are linear, homogenous functions of the capital and labor devoted to productive and unproductive activities, respectively. These can be written:

$$Q = q(K_q, L_q) \text{ and} \tag{4.2}$$

$$R = r(K_r, L_r). \tag{4.3}$$

Subject to the constraints that capital used for rent-seeking and capital used for productive purposes total to all available capital, and that labor used for rent-seeking and labor used for productive uses total to all available labor, such that

$$K = K_q + K_r \text{ and}$$

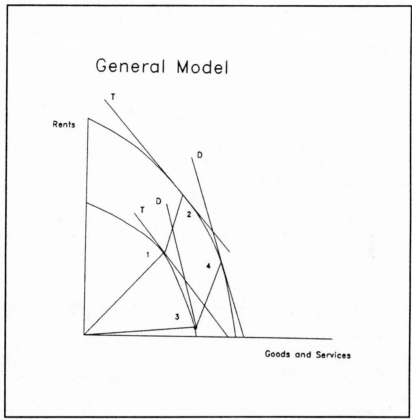

Figure 4.1

$$L = L_q + L_r,$$

where K and L are total available capital and labor, and where the subscripts $_q$ and $_r$ refer to capital and labor devoted to productive and rent-seeking uses, respectively.

The $MRTS_{k,l}$ (i.e., the marginal rate of technical substitution of the factors K and L in the production of Q or in the pursuit of R) for either Q or R can be expressed, generally,

$$MRTS^i_{k,l} = -\delta K/\delta L = MP_{l,i}/MP_{k,i},$$

where i is either Q or R, respectively. In the two sector model here efficiency (in the sense that returns to factors are equalized) would be attained when

$$-\delta K/\delta L = MP_{l,q}/MP_{k,q} = MP_{l,r}/MP_{k,r}.$$

The slope of the transformation curve, figure 4.1, is the Marginal Rate of Transformation, $MRT_{R,Q} = -\delta R/\delta Q$.

Reducing the amount of rent-seeking releases factors of production

$$\delta L_q(MP_l) + \delta K_q(MP_k).$$

Increasing rent-seeking will reduce the factors dedicated to production by the amount

$$\delta L_r(MR_l) + \delta K_r(MR_k).$$

If the factors are to be fully employed then the quantities of each factor released by one activity must be equal to the factors being increased for the other activity

$$-\delta L_r = +\delta L_q \text{ and}$$

$$-\delta K_r = +\delta K_q.$$

The total differentiation of the transformation curve yields the slope of the transformation curve

$$\frac{\delta R}{\delta Q} = \frac{\delta L_r(MR_l) + \delta K_r(MR_k)}{\delta L_q(MP_l) + \delta K_q(MP_k)}$$

To maximize the use of resources the economy must stay on the transformation curve, not inside it. This implies that

$$(\textit{slope of isoquant Q}) = \frac{MP_l}{MP_k} = \frac{MR_l}{MR_k} = (\textit{slope of isoquant R}) \qquad (4.4)$$

Therefore

$$MP_l = MP_k \frac{MR_l}{MR_k} \tag{4.5}$$

and

$$MR_l = MR_k \frac{MP_l}{MP_k} \tag{4.6}$$

Dividing the total differential by δL_r, when $\delta L_r = - \delta L_q$, yields

$$-\frac{\delta R}{\delta Q} = \frac{MR_l + MR_k (\delta K_r / \delta L_r)}{-MP_k - MP_k (\delta K_q / \delta L_q)} \tag{4.7}$$

Substituting (4.5) and (4.6) into (4.7) we get

$$-\frac{\delta R}{\delta Q} = \frac{MR_k \{ \dfrac{MP_l}{MP_k} + \dfrac{\delta K_l}{\delta L_k} \}}{-MP_k \{ \dfrac{MR_1}{MR_k} + \dfrac{\delta K_q}{\delta L_q} \}}$$

From equation (4.1) we know that the first terms in the top and bottom brackets are equal. Also, since $\delta K_r = \delta K_q$, the second terms in the top and bottom brackets are equal.:

$$-\frac{\delta R}{\delta Q} = \frac{MR_k}{MP_k}$$

and, similarly

Therefore, the slope of the transformation curve is

$$-\frac{\delta R}{\delta Q} = \frac{MR_l}{MP_l}$$

$$-\frac{\delta R}{\delta Q} = \frac{MR_k}{MP_k} = \frac{MR_l}{MP_l}$$

The optimal combination of rent-seeking and productive activities, is that which yields the individual the highest return. He has a choice of gaining income from rent-seeking or from production of goods and services. The economic agent is indifferent as to the source of income, i.e., income from rent is equivalent to income from producing goods and services. In Chapter 3 the costs of rent-seeking facing rent-seekers under various regimes were discussed. Individuals face the objective function:

Y = Q + (1-c)R,

where Y is income from rents or production of goods and services, and c is the institutional cost of rent-seeking facing rent-seekers from figure 3.1,[2] $0<c<1$. This can be manipulated:[3] This formulation refers only to the decision facing individuals or institutions. It cannot hold in the aggregate since all distributions are from Q only. However, at the microeconomic level this formulation is a valid representation of the choices available between rent-seeking or producing goods and services.

Y = Q + (1-c)R

(Y - Q)/(1-c) = R

$\delta R/\delta Q = -1/(1-c)$.   (4.8)

When the individual seeks to maximize his private income from both sources (i.e., from rent-seeking and productive activity) he maximizes the income function Y = Q + (1-c)R, which can be solved by setting dY = 0, yielding an isoreturn line, which is a straight line having the slope $-1/(1-c)$. If c equals zero then marginal rent will be equal to marginal product. Where c is greater than zero then marginal rent will be greater than marginal product, for instance, say $c = .2$, then $\delta R/\delta Q = -1/.8$.

Where the transformation curve and the isoreturn line are tangent this yields an equilibrium position (i.e., where the net returns from rent-seeking and productive use of resources are equalized). These two lines are tangent when

$$MR_i = (1-c)MP_i \qquad (4.9)$$

where i refers to either capital or labor. For instance, if there is a unit cost to rent-seeking then the before cost return to rent-seeking must be higher than the return to productive activity in order for any rent-seeking to be worthwhile.

In figure 4.1 the isoreturn line T is not as steep as isoreturn line D since it represents a regime with little political pluralism and hence low institutional costs of rent-seeking for rent-seekers. Thus, point 1 implies a higher ratio of rents to goods and services than does point 3.

If we hold population (and the labor force) constant but increase capital stock the transformation curve shifts in a non-homothetic manner, rising more on the Y-axis than it moves out on the X-axis. This non-homothetic shift occurs because of the income elasticity of rents discussed in Chapter 3. This income elasticity of rents implies that as income rises rent opportunities also rise even without a concomitant increase in resources devoted to rent-seeking. Hence, the "production" of rents at any given level becomes a bit cheaper in terms of the opportunity cost of resources that can be used for productive purposes.

A movement from point 3 to 4 in figure 4.1 implies an increase in goods and services as well as a rise in rents. From a neo-classical point of view the increase in goods and services is all that would be used in calculating the return to capital. Clearly the return to capital must include the rents the capital stock can also generate. If there were no return to such capital there would be no rent-seeking.

From figure 4.1 and equations (4.1) through (4.9), a general, rent-augmented growth model can be specified, indicating movement from one transformation curve out to another:

$$\Delta U = \Delta Q + \Delta R = \alpha + MR_l(1-c)\Delta L_q + MR_l\Delta L_r$$
$$+ MR_k(1-c)\Delta K_k + MR_kK_r \qquad (4.10)$$

where
- Δ is the first difference operator
- Q represents goods and services of the productive sector, which will be indicated by GDP in 1980 US dollars, and
- R is the level of rents.
- U is the total of output of real goods and services and rents, and for the sake of giving this variable a name, we can refer to it as "potential output," since the formulation here implies that if all resources were used for the production of goods and services and none were devoted to rent-seeking then Q would equal U.

In order to derive an estimable equation that will yield useful insights it is necessary to separate the growth in resources devoted to productive activities from those used productively. Unfortunately, the separation cannot be made from observations. To make a useful approximation it is necessary to invoke some strong assumptions.

In the first instance, if we assume that the ratio of rents to output (R/Q) remains fairly constant for "small" changes in R and Q,[4] then it can also be assumed that will also remain in proportion, i.e., the ratio MP_k/MR_l remains constant for "small" changes in R and Q.[5] It follows, rather tenuously, then that we can assume that the share of the increases in resources going to a sector is equal to the ratio of the marginal product to the marginal rent then

$$\Delta L_q = (MP/MR)\Delta L, \text{ and } \Delta L_r = (1-MP/MR)\Delta L.$$

And keeping in mind from equation (4.9) that $MP = MR(1-c)$, then

$$\Delta L = \{MR(1-c)/MR\}\Delta L + \{1-[MR(1-c)/MR\}\Delta L \text{ and}$$

$$MP\Delta L_q + MR\Delta L_r$$

$$= MP\{MR(1-c)/MR\}\Delta L + MR\{1-[MR(1-c)/MR]\}\Delta L$$

$$= MP(1-c)\Delta L + MR\{1-1-c\}\Delta L$$

$$= MP(1-c)\Delta L + MR(-c)\Delta L$$

substituting $MR(1-c)$ into MP

$$= MR(1-c)^2\Delta L + MR(-c)\Delta L$$

$$= MR(1+c^2-3c)\Delta L \qquad (4.11)$$

Let $c^2-3c = -C$, which is less than zero, i.e., $C>0$, since $0<c<1$.

Altering equation (4.10) to reflect equation (4.11) yields

$$\Delta U = \Delta Q+\Delta R = \alpha + MR_l(1-C)\Delta L + MR_k(1-C)\Delta K \qquad (4.12)$$

which is the major equation of the rent-augmented growth model.

Rent-seeking has important implications for incentives to invest. Since the return to rent-seeking must be paid out of the produce of the productive activities of other factors rent-seeking can be seen as a "rent tax" on factors. This can be illustrated using Euler's theorem[6] total factor utilization implies distribution of returns according to marginal products and factor shares. However, since some portion of factors are used for non-productive purposes while only the fruit of factors used productively is available for distribution Euler's theorem cannot attain in rent-seeking economies. If it did hold, and, for the sake of simplicity, the only factor were capital, then

$$U = Q+R = MPK_q + MRK_r.$$

However, we know from equation (4.9) that $MR = MP/(1-c)$, therefore

$$U = Q+R = MPK_q + \{MP/(1-c)\}K_r. \qquad (4.13)$$

This cannot hold since rents are merely redistributions of Q. Therefore, the total that can be distributed cannot exceed Q.

Equation (4.3) can be rewritten

$$Q(1+R/Q) = MPK_q + \{MP/(1-c)\}K_r.$$

Let $R/Q = \tau$, and divide both sides of this equation by $(1+\tau)$

$$Q = \{MP/(1+\tau)\}K_q + \{MP/(1-c)/(1+\tau)\}K_r. \qquad (4.14)$$

Thus, the larger the share of rent-seeking in an economy the lower the returns to factors, whether these factors are used for rent-seeking or for productive purposes. Quite obviously capital must receive less than its marginal product in rent-seeking economies. Indeed, in an economy where rents come to 20% of GDP (a near median value for Africa, as shown in Appendix 1) the net return to factors will be 20% below their marginal products. We should expect investment therefore to be inversely related to the share of rents in GDP.

The model is useful not only in that it shows that individuals have a choice between using resources productively and non-productively, but also because it points out an error in variables that has biased estimates of capital's efficiency. In 1957 Milton Friedman showed that if consumption were a linear function of permanent rather than of observed income then the marginal propensity to consume would be greater than what was observable under the absolute income hypothesis of consumption. Similarly, the rent-augmented model indicates that the if investment is devoted to both production and rent-seeking then its efficiency should be measured in terms of its gross rate of return,[7] which is the inverse of the capital-output ratio not as Q/I but instead as (Q+R)/I. The importance of this distinction is that while some analysts have found capital output ratios (actually, incremental capital output ratios, or ICORs) to be quite large in Africa,[8] (in some cases ICORs exceed 100) these large ICORs, and their implied very low social rates of return, need to be explained since, prima faci, they are not consistent with neo-classical theory.[9] figure 4.2 illustrates the error in variables bias and its relevance to the return to capital.

Before this analysis can proceed to the estimation stage it is necessary to show how rents have been calculated. This is done in the next section.

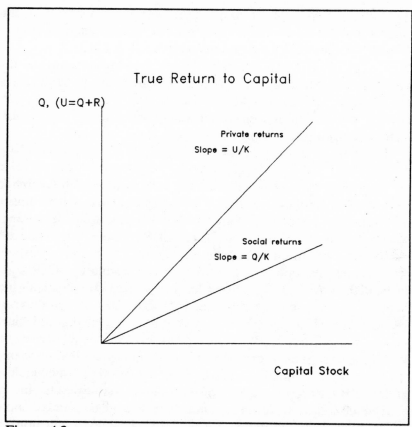

True Return to Capital

Q, (U=Q+R)

Private returns
Slope = U/K

Social returns
Slope = Q/K

Capital Stock

Figure 4.2

Calculating Rents

Although the rent-augmented growth model includes the term (R), aggregate rents, there is no statistical system reporting these aggregate rents. In this section I suggest methodologies for calculating rents, combining economic theory with minimal data availability. When the aim is to aggregate rents for a large number of countries the difficulties grow exponentially. Considering the database for Africa the task seems almost impossible. However, by making a few simplifying assumptions and by concentrating on the rents related to the major policy issues[10] some aggregate calculations can be ventured.[11]

Only rents are calculated, the dead weight losses are sufficiently small and can be ignored.[12] All rents will be calculated in terms of 1980 US dollars. Five major rents will be calculated in the areas of: trade protection (revenue-seeking by government and protection of domestic manufacturing), agricultural monopsonistic markets, foreign exchange overvaluation, and non-market allocation of capital. The size of government is treated separately, since its rent generation cannot be aggregated in the same way as these.

These are elaborated below.

Trade Protection. The imposition of import duties in the search for government revenues gives rise to smuggling and costs of enforcement and creates a rent for domestic factors producing the import substituting commodities. In figure 4.3 S_p is the supply curve of domestically produced manufactures.

S_d represents total supply of domestically produced and smuggled in manufactures. Q_t-Q_d is total legal imports. Q_d-Q_p is smuggled imports. I assume here, for simplicity sake, that smuggled goods crowd out legally imported goods without reducing the domestic price. Q_p-0 is domestically produced manufactures. Area A is rent granted to domestic manufacturers; C is profits of smuggling; E is total tariff revenue to government. Areas B, D, and F are dead-weight losses, although B may represent part of the return to smugglers.

The entire tariff revenue, area E, is included as the rent to government from the imposition of tariff. Dividing total tariffs by total imports into a country yields an effective tariff rate, which can be used to estimate t, where

$$t = (P_d\text{-}P_w)/P_w.$$

Assuming the rate of tariff only applies to manufactures and only domestic manufactures receive protection, the total value of domestic manufactures can serve as a proxy for H. Area B is not part of the manufacturers' total value added but will be smaller the more inelastic is domestic manufacturer's supply function. An approximation of area A is to multiply the proxy value for t by the proxy value for H (which is total value-added of manufacturing),   A = tH - B, although B will be ignored since it is unobservable and its precise meaning is elusive.[13]

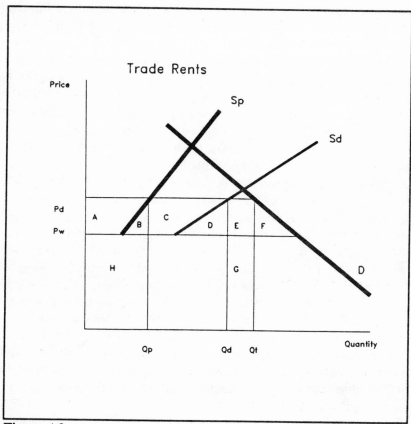

Figure 4.3

Although total value-added in manufactures is probably a fairly accurate proxy for H, the proxy for t is an understatement. Since t is calculated by dividing total tariffs by total imports and since some imports (such as food and some capital goods) are not taxed or are taxed at a lower rate this t must be too small. For instance, t = total tariff revenue ÷ total imports, which is less than total tariff revenue ÷ imports of dutiable goods, since dutiable goods will be less than total imports.

Since the distortions of trade intervention through quantitative restrictions is not included in this calculation we can rest fairly comfortably that any calculation of trade protection created rents is understated.

Agriculture. Studies of agriculture in LDCs often measure price distortions by the nominal protection coefficient (NPC), calculated as the ratio of farm prices to the international price of the agricultural export at current official exchange rates but after adjustment for international and domestic transport and marketing costs.[14] The difference between the NPC and the value 1 represents either the implicit subsidy or the implicit tax on agricultural export producers (if the NPC is less than one this implies a monopsonistic tax is imposed on agricultural export producers, whereas when the NPC is greater than one agricultural production is being subsidized) arising from price controls and monopsonistic domination by agricultural marketing boards.   Since subsidization tends to occur more often from general fluctuations in world prices and domestic costs rather than from intent to provide farmers with subsidies (although this does happen from time to time) only the implicit tax will be included. The calculation of rent is (1-NPC) multiplied by the value of the agricultural export.

Similar rents exist for domestically consumed agricultural products but data are not available.   Also, much agricultural produce is smuggled out of the country and does not get included in official statistics but bears the costs of avoiding enforcement and detection. The calculations here will only allow assessment of rents on one or two major commodities for most of the countries. Several countries may produce more than this limited number of cash crops, but NPCs are unavailable for them.

Foreign Exchange. The premium of the black market rate versus the official rate of exchange multiplied by the amount of exports in U.S. dollars will serve as the measure of rent available from receiving foreign exchange allocations. The calculation is made by multiplying the rent rate of 1 - (official/black market exchange rate) by the amount of exports denominated in U.S. dollars. For example, if the official exchange rate were one kwacha to one dollar (1:1) while the black market rate were 3:1, then an importer receiving an allocation of $100 in foreign exchange would be receiving a rent equivalent to $66.66 = $100(1-1/3).

The trend of average black market to official market exchange rates in Africa from 1970 to 1985 is shown in figure 4.4.

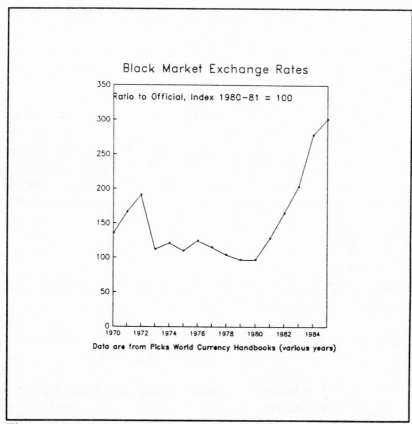

Figure 4.4

<u>Non-Market Allocation of Capital.</u> This rent is given by the negative value of the below zero real interest rate multiplied by domestic credit. This measure is likely to overstate the actual rents generated, since it is likely that only a portion of domestic credit will be allocated at negative real interest rates.[15] For the empirical testing in this chapter R1 was used, since it contains the most information.

<u>Aggregate Rents.</u> The sum of the rent calculations make up the aggregate rents analyzed in this paper.

Empirical Equations

<u>General Model.</u> Equation (4.12) is the main equation representing the major aspects of the rent-augmented growth model. It is repeated here.

$$\Delta U = \Delta Q + \Delta R = \alpha + MR_l(1-C)\Delta L + MR_k(1-C)\Delta K \qquad (4.12)$$

Equation (4.12) requires a few modifications before empirical analysis can be performed. The first is to specify the variable C. We can posit that C is a positive linear function of the degree of political pluralism, which is a proxy for the degree of institutional competition:

$$C = \Phi RD,$$

where RD indicates the degree of political pluralism. This specification is substituted into equation (4.12).

$$\Delta U = \Delta Q + \Delta R = \alpha + MR_l(1-\Phi RD)\Delta L + MR_k(1-\Phi RD)\Delta K \qquad (4.15)$$

Additionally, Chapter 2 discussed the inclusion of an indicator of the growth in the government sector in many empirical models as well as an indicator of investment in human capital. These can also be included into the empirical model here

$$\Delta U = \Delta Q + \Delta R = \alpha + MR_l(1-\Phi RD)\Delta L + MR_k(1-\Phi RD)\Delta K$$
$$+ \gamma \Delta G + \epsilon NIH \qquad (4.16)$$

where
G is total government spending, and
NIH is growth in government spending on education.

The discussions of non-market decision making in Chapter 3 lead us to expect that γ would be negative, however, results of other empirically tested growth models have been mixed. On the one hand, government spending is inefficient, while on the other hand, it provides for important social services and provides social overhead capital. The sign of ϵ should be positive as we should expect that investment in education would enhance growth.

By dividing equation (4.16) by Q we can eliminate the heteroscedasticity that may arise due to the size of these economies.

In order to derive an empirically interesting model that yields results that can easily be interpreted it is necessary to make some further manipulations of the basic model and to invoke an assumption that has explicitly been made by Bruno (1968) and Feder (1983), but which seems to have implicitly been made by others. Following Bruno (1968) and also Feder (1983) we can substitute the growth rate of the labor force for the change in labor force divided by GDP. Bruno suggests this specification when there is disequilibrium since he posits that the marginal productivity of labor is a linear function of the average productivity. Bruno suggests that the marginal wage rate will not be equated to the marginal product of labor in less developed countries, except perhaps over the long run, due to either disequilibrium or imperfections in factor markets. He suggests that in many countries the transfer of workers from the country-side into urban areas involves a large boost in labor's earnings beyond that warranted by productivity. He refers to this as part of the costs of urbanization. Since Bruno first wrote this piece in 1968 there have been developments in rural-urban migration theories, such as Todaro (1977), that perhaps better explain the higher remuneration of labor in high unemployment plagued African cities. Nonetheless, Bruno finds some empirical validation for his assumption in estimating a growth model for Israel. Others seem to implicitly assume the same disequilibrium. For instance, Grier and Tullock (1989) and Meguire (1985) present models where the rate of growth of GDP is a function of the rate of growth of the labor force and the investment-GDP ratio. Without the Bruno assumption, or something similar, this specification cannot be derived from the usual family of linear, homogenous production functions where output is a function of labor and capital. Thus, if $MP_l = \sigma AP_l$, then $MP_l = \sigma Q/L$.

Therefore, we can alter the labor specification in equation (4.16) adding in $\sigma Q/L$, and letting $MR_l = \psi(Q/L)$, letting $\beta = \sigma\psi$, and dividing both sides by Q, we get

$$\Delta U/Q = \alpha + \beta(1-\Phi RD)\Delta L/L + MR_k(1-\Phi RD)\Delta K/Q$$
$$+ \gamma\Delta G/Q + \epsilon\Delta NIH/Q$$

Multiplying by Q/ΔL yields

$$\Delta U/\Delta L = f + \beta(1\text{-}\Phi RD)Q/L + MR_k(1\text{-}\Phi RD)\Delta K/\Delta L$$
$$+ \gamma\Delta G/\Delta L + \epsilon NIH/\Delta L$$

Which implies that the marginal U (potential product) of labor is a function of the average product of labor and the incremental capital-labor ratio, among other things. It seems quite reasonable to expect that the marginal U of labor should rise with the incremental capital-labor ratio. If we assume that the average product of labor is a good proxy for the capital-labor ratio, as would be implied in a Cobb-Douglas production function, then we should expect that the marginal U of labor would be inversely associated with the average product of labor or the capital-labor ratio. For example, let $Q = K^\alpha L^{1-\alpha}$, where Q is output of goods and services, K is capital and L is labor, and $0<\alpha<1$. It can be shown that average product per worker is a non-linear function of the capital-labor ratio, i.e., dividing both sides of the production function by L yields $Q/L = (K/L)^\alpha$, and therefore, in a rough sense, the average product for labor may serve as a proxy for the capital-labor ratio.

$$\Delta U/\Delta L = f + \beta(1\text{-}\Phi RD)Q/L + MR_k(1\text{-}\Phi RD)\Delta K/\Delta L$$
$$+ \gamma\Delta G/\Delta L + \epsilon NIH/\Delta L + v \qquad (4.17)*$$

where v is an error term. Equation (4.17)* can be estimated using non-linear least squares.

Similarly, we can ignore the Bruno specification, as an alternative, but still dividing by Q and adding PCY to equation (4.16) will yield a new estimable equation (4.18)*.

The theory of competitive rent-seeking suggests that rent-seeking will be higher where per capita incomes are higher. On the other hand, neo-classical growth models imply that due to diminishing returns to capital incomes will converge and therefore per capita income should be negatively correlated with economic growth. The sign of per capita income in this equation will be fairly ambiguous. However, if the rent-seeking impact should overshadow the convergence impact then the sign will be positive. If the convergence impact overshadows the rent-seeking impact then the sign will be negative. Additionally, since the average product of labor, which is nearly the same as per capita income, is already in the equation and can already indicate the appearance of convergence, this creates additional statistical difficulties. If neither impact overshadows the other then the coefficient will not be significantly different from zero, which could also indicate that this indicator is irrelevant to this specification. Despite these ambiguities per capita income is, nonetheless, included, since it is theoretically necessary. Adding per capita income (PCY) then yields

$$\Delta U/Q = \alpha + MR_l(1\text{-}\Phi RD)\Delta L/Q + MR_k(1\text{-}\Phi RD)\Delta K/Q$$
$$+ \gamma \Delta G/Q + \epsilon \Delta NIH/Q + \phi PCY + u \qquad (4.18)*$$

where u is an error term and which can be estimated using NLS.

Rent-Augmented vs. the Neo-classical Model. Equation (4.18)* cannot be directly compared to the neo-classical model. However, the neo-classical model can be altered somewhat to include the rent variable. This can be done by using general neo-classical specifications of the structural variables that have an effect on growth.

The simple neo-classical model has economic growth as a function of the growth of capital and labor

$$\Delta Q = \delta_0 + \delta_1 \Delta L + \delta_2 \Delta K.$$

Dividing this by Q

$$\Delta Q/Q = \delta_0 + \delta_1 \Delta L/Q + \delta_2 \Delta K/Q.$$

Now adding in the share of government spending in the economy, as well as RD, which some have used (for instance, Barro 1989a&b) to indicate property rights, yields

$$\Delta Q/Q = \delta_0 + \delta_1 \Delta L/Q$$
$$+ \delta_2 \Delta K/Q + \delta_3 G/Q + \delta_4 RD + u \qquad (4.19)*.$$

The share of rents in the economy can be added to (4.19)* to yield

$$\Delta Q/Q = \alpha_0 + \alpha_1 L/Q + \alpha_2 \Delta K/Q + \alpha_3 G/Q$$
$$+ \alpha_4 RD + \alpha_5 R/Q + \epsilon \qquad 4.20)*$$

Where u and ϵ are error terms.

These two specifications can be estimated and compared.

Rent-Seeking and the Rate of Return. Since returns to rent-seekers are paid out of the fruit of productive labor and capital it follows that productive labor and capital must be remunerated by less than the amount of their contribution to output. Growth comes not only from the rate of investment (and growth in other resources) but also from the returns to investment (and to other resources). From equation (4.14) we should expect that the rate of return to capital will be inversely related to the ratio of rents in the economy. (4.14) is repeated

$$Q = \{MP/(1+\tau)\}K_q + \{MP/(1-c)/(1+\tau)\}K_r \qquad (4.14)$$

where K refers to all resources.

In addition, factors other than the degree of rent-seeking will also affect investment. For instance, total investment includes both private and public sector investment.[16] Public investment is often taken for political and social reasons rather than for economic reasons, therefore the greater the share of public investment in total investment the lower rate of return to investment will be. The size of government in the economy will be positively related to the rate of public sector investment since a larger overall budget can allow greater capital expenditure. Since there is no information about public sector investment total government spending will be used as a proxy, where it is assumed that public sector spending is some fraction of total government spending. There is no specific evidence that this is true in Africa. However, it is important that this proxy be included in this specification since it is quite well known that public sector spending, especially during the 1980s, has made up the majority of total investment in most African countries. Since data on public vs. private sector investment spending are not available this is suggested as a first approximation. So, although the size of the public sector might be positively related to the rate of aggregate investment the inefficiency of the public sector should lead us to expect the public sector's size to be negatively related to the the productivity of investment. The degree of political pluralism can also be expected to have a positive impact on the rate of return since it raises the costs of rent-seeking, is an indicator of property rights, and may be associated with greater political stability. Shocks, such as riots, droughts, and coups d'etat, can be expected to harm the rate of return since they often destroy assets or shut down the economy for some time, thus causing assets to lie idle. Also, in underdeveloped economies, such as in Africa, improvements in the international terms of trade can be expected to provide opportunities for investment in the export sector, while declining terms of trade can be expected to be associated with declining investment.

A special aspect of African societies is their lack of social or cultural homogeneity. To the extent that the lack of cultural homogeneity (HOM) may lead to lobbying for public investment based on other than economic grounds (for instance, nation building, regional integration, political peace making, etc.) this will lower the rate of return to public investment, although it may have little impact on the overall rate of public investment since public investment is undertaken for policy reasons. There are competing indices of homogeneity[17] but I have selected the number of identifiable languages (the more languages the less heterogeneous the society) since this is the most clear cut of the competing indices and is less subjective in measurement.[18]

If these economies exhibit diminishing returns then the rate of return to investment should be lower where the capital labor ratio is higher. Since there is no information on capital stock in Africa, a proxy for this is output per laborer, under the assumption that output per laborer is largely a function of capital per laborer. Thus, the rate of return on investment will be negatively related to output per laborer (Q/L).

A general relationship between these factors and the rate of return is posited

$$RETURN = r_0 + r_1 HOM + r_2 R/Q + r_3 G/Q$$
$$+ r_4 SHOCK + r_5 Q/L + r_6 RD + r_7 NIH/Q + \gamma \quad (4.21)*$$

where

RETURN is the gross social rate of return on investment, measured as the change in output (Q) over investment, $\Delta Q/I$,

HOM is the degree of cultural homogeneity, indicated by the inverse of the number of indigenous languages spoken in country t, the sign of which should be positive, under the expectation that the more homogeneous the society the less petitioning of government for uneconomic public investment programs,

R/Q is the ratio of rents to GDP, rents measurement has already been discussed, and the expected sign is negative,

G/Q is the ratio of the government sector size (total central government expenditures) to GDP, and the expected sign is negative since government not only is positively associated with rent-seeking, which reduces returns, but also because the larger government is the larger we should expect government's share in total investment to be, and given the likely uneconomic portfolios of government investment programs we should expect the sign to be negative,

SHOCK is the indicator of natural and man made, but not economic, negative shocks, as discussed in Appendix 2, shocks can destroy assets and as such lower their returns, additionally, civil disturbances may encourage people to hide their assets and hence keep them unproductive until the situation stabilizes, hence the sign should be negative,

RD is the indicator of the degree of political pluralism, inverted from Gastil (1987) as discussed in Chapter 3, and the sign should be positive,

NIH represents net investment in human capital, indicated by the average change in real education spending by central government, as discussed in Appendix 2, since Lucas leads us to expect that investment in human capital yields the externality of raising the productivity of other factors, the sign should be positive, and

γ is an error term.

Similarly, we can expect that the same factors that affect the rate of return might also affect the rate of investment, although not necessarily in the same way. For instance, although government size might be expected to lower the rate of return to investment, because government is the major source of investment funds in most African countries. Remember, investment spending data are not broken down

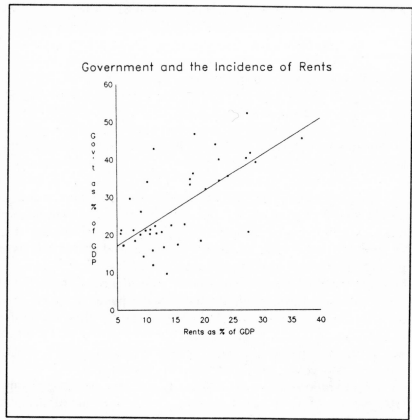

Figure 4.5

between private and public sector spending. the larger is government the more investment spending should be expected. Additionally, improvements in the terms of trade should attract new investment to the export sector, especially foreign investment. Thus, the investment function should also include the terms of trade adjuster (TT) which is calculated by weighting the growth in the international terms of trade by the proportion of exports in GDP. Also, the 1980s saw a deterioration in the availability of international liquidity. To control for the period of short international lending I include the TIME variable which is equal to 0 for the first time period data (1975-81) and 1 for the second time period data (1981-87). Thus, an investment function can be expressed

$$\Delta K/Q = i_0 + i_1 HOM + i_2 R/Q + i_3 G/Q + i_4 SHOCK$$
$$+ i_5 Q/L + i_6 RD + i_7 NIH/Q + i_8 TT$$
$$+ i_9 TIME + \alpha \qquad (4.22)^*$$

where $\underline{TT}$ is the terms of trade adjuster,
$\underline{TIME}$ is the time variable $\{0 = 1975\text{-}81, 1 = 1981\text{-}87\}$, and
$\underline{\alpha}$ is an error term.

Equations $(4.21)^*$ and $(4.22)^*$ can both be estimated using ordinary least squares.

Incidence of Rent: The general model as well as the discussion of rent-seeking in Chapter 3 lead us to expect that rents will be larger relative to the rest of the economy where per capita incomes are greater, where the government sector is larger and where there is less political freedom.   Figure 4.5 indicates an apparent relationship between the size of government and the incidence of rents. Figure 4.6 indicates the positive relationship between per capita incomes and the size of rents relative to GDP. Two equations can be specified. In the first, growth in rents is a function of growth in Q and G, as well as of investment, since investment is used for both productive uses and rent-seeking, and to the degree of political pluralism. In the second, the ratio of rents to GDP is a function of the government to GDP ratio, per capita income, the degree of political pluralism, and degree of homogeneity, since greater interest group participation might be expected to lead to more lobbying for government services and protection. These two incidence equations are specified:

$$\Delta R/Q = \pi_0 + \pi_1 \Delta Q/Q + \pi_2 G/Q + \pi_3 RD + \pi_4 HOM$$
$$+ \pi_5 PCY + \pi_6 R/Q + \tau \qquad (4.23)^*$$

and

$$R/Q = f_0 + f_1 G/Q + f_2 PCY + f_3 RD + f_4 HOM + \phi \qquad (4.24)^*$$

These equations can be estimated using ordinary least squares.

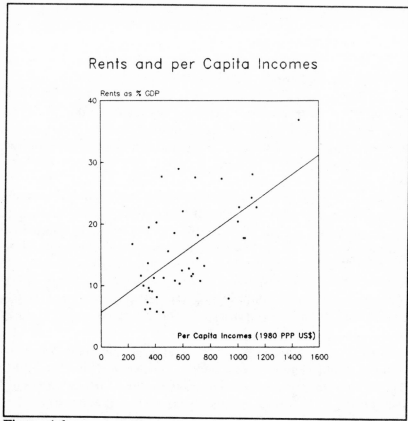

Figure 4.6

Methods and Estimations

The hypotheses at the end of Chapter 3 led to the construction of the general, rent-augmented model. The model's specification is consistent with those hypotheses. All regressions and correlations are estimated using all available data, since this is the most prudent use of limited data. However, when comparing the rent-augmented structural model to that of the neo-classical model, the same sample set will be used. This restricts the degrees of freedom in the neo-classical test but allows direct comparison.

General Model (NLS and OLS). The estimable equations of part C can be estimated by using regression methods. Repeating

$$\Delta U/\Delta L = f + \beta(1-\Phi RD)Q/L + MR_k(1-\Phi RD)\Delta K/\Delta L$$
$$+ \gamma\Delta G/\Delta L + \epsilon NIH/\Delta L + \phi PCY + v \qquad (4.17)^*$$

where v is an error term, can be estimated using non-linear least squares. Non-linear least squares (NLS) can be used to estimate the equation's parameters since the equation is non-linear in its variables. The advantage of using NLS over ordinary least squares (OLS) is that NLS will generate a standard error -- and a t-statistic -- for Φ, whereas OLS will estimate $\beta\Phi$ and $MR_k\Phi$ as individual parameters. While the results are essentially identical, OLS will not generate the standard error for Φ and testing of Φ and testing for the significance of the parameter would have to be less direct.[19]

Thus $(4.17)^*$ can be factored out to allow OLS

$$\Delta U/\Delta L = f + \beta Q/L - \beta\Phi RDQ/L + MR_k\Delta K/\Delta L + MR_k\Phi RD\Delta K/\Delta L$$
$$+ \gamma\Delta G/\Delta L + \epsilon NIH/\Delta L + \phi PCY + v \qquad (4.25)^*$$

NLS will also allow us to set the restriction that Φ be the same for either capital or labor, or to let Φ's value be determined by the data. These two regressions, the restricted and unrestricted, can be compared by comparison of the adjusted R^2s and F-statistics.

Finding the coefficient of Φ to be significantly greater than zero would tend to confirm hypothesis 2 of Chapter 2, which is that rent-seeking is costlier to the rent-seeker where institutional competition for rents is greater. Similarly, hypothesis 1, which is the converse of hypothesis 2, would also confirmed.

To the extent that the overall equations $(4.17)^*$ and $(4.25)^*$ meet goodness of fit criteria, this would tend to confirm the fifth hypothesis, which is that rent-seeking diverts resources from productive activity and therefore slows growth.

Testing for Endogeneity. Easterly and Wetzel (1989) suggested that two-stage least squares (TSLS) might need to be used for their growth model data "in order to account for the fact that improved growth is likely to have an impact on investment and export performance."

They ran TSLS on their data and found that the coefficients for these two variables were smaller than when OLS was used, but that they were still significant. Easterly and Wetzel did not actually test for endogeneity (or exogeneity). Most of the other empirical literature reviewed in chapter 2 used only OLS.

Before proceeding to estimate the major equations of this model it is necessary to test for investment's endogeneity. The Hausman test[20] will allow to test for endogeneity. The first step is to define the major model equation to be estimated. In this case we will use the OLS version of the general model, i.e., equation (4.25)*. Next, define the first stage equation for determining the suspected endogenous variable, in this case $\Delta K/\Delta L$. Since equation (4.22)* already specifies an investment function we need only modify it slightly by changing R/Q to R/ΔL, G/Q to G/ΔL, and NIH/Q to NIH/ΔL. The second stage then is to save the residual term from this first stage and include it with all the other variables into the next step estimation of equation (4.22)*. If the coefficient of this residual term is not significantly greater than zero then we can accept that investment is NOT endogenously determined and that OLS would yield consistent estimators for (4.22)*, and that NLS would yield unbiased estimators for (4.17)*.

More formally: the test is to determine if there is a significant difference between the coefficient of observed investment and the instrumental variable. For example, let the true coefficient of investment be β and the coefficient for the instrumental variable be equal to β and another θ, then to test if the equation is misspecified the null hypothesis would be

$$H_0: \Theta = \beta,$$
$$H_A: \Theta \neq \beta.$$

The independent variable without specification error can be expressed as X' = X^* - u, where X' is the observed value of the correct variable X, X^* is the vector of fitted values from the first stage regression and ε represents the residuals of that regression, then the testing regression for the significance of the error in specification

$$Y = c + \beta X + \Theta \varepsilon + u, \text{ which is equivalent to}$$
$$Y = c + \beta X' + (\Theta - \beta)\varepsilon + u.$$

The test then of the significance of error in the suspected variable is if the coefficient of ϵ is significantly different than zero. This is presented in table 4.1 using the t-test.

Rent-Augmented versus the Neo-classical Model. Estimating equations (4.19)* and (4.20)* can be done with OLS. The same sample sets will be used for both equations. There is an additional problem. The rent-seeking theories developed in this dissertation lead us to expect that R/Q and G/Q would be correlated. Also, since R/Q is correlated with G/Q, and as has been shown elsewhere G/Q is correlated with PCY, and PCY is correlated with RD, then we are likely to find difficulties of multicollinearity. One method for addressing this problem is to present a number of equations dropping various variables and seeing how this affects the overall estimation and the estimated coefficients. For instance, from estimable equations (4.19) and (4.20), we can see how the inclusion/deletion of the rent variable (R/Q) improves the overall equation's goodness of fit (by comparing the adjusted R^2s) and inspect the changes in coefficients and t-statistics.

$$\Delta Q/Q = \delta_0 + \delta_1 \Delta L/Q + \delta_2 \Delta K/Q + \delta_3 G/Q$$
$$+ \delta_4 RD + u \qquad\qquad (4.19)^*.$$

$$\Delta Q/Q = \alpha_0 + \alpha_1 L/Q + \alpha_2 \Delta K/Q + \alpha_3 G/Q$$
$$+ \delta_4 RD + \alpha_5 R/Q + \epsilon \qquad\qquad (4.20)^*.$$

If $\alpha_5 < 0$, this would tends to confirm the hypothesis that rent-seeking diverts resources from productive uses and slows growth. However, this can only be accepted if (4.20)* significantly improves the overall explanation of the variance in $\Delta Q/Q$ compared to (4.19)*. This comparison can be made by seeing if there is much change in the adjusted R^2.

Treatment of Multicollinearity. Multicollinearity is the linear dependence of two or more of the independent variables. Perfect collinearity among independent variables is easily detected since it prevents the use of OLS since the rank of the matrix of the independent variables is less than the number of independent variables (i.e., the **X** matrix and hence the **X'X** are not full rank and therefore cannot be inverted). Less than perfect collinearity, in a sense, is more of a problem than perfect collinearity since the regression can be run but the resultant errors may be "too large" to indicate significance even when the relationship posited is in fact valid.

The rent-seeking theory in this dissertation suggests that rent-seeking is positively associated with the size of government and per capita incomes, while being negatively associated with the degree of political pluralism. On the other hand, it has been shown that in Africa the tendency has been that government size tends to rise more than proportionately with incomes. Also, the rent-seeking theory leads us to expect that there will be greater growth in GDP in the countries where political pluralism is greater. Table A.2 in the Appendix indicates high, positive correlation among R/Q, PCY, RD, and G/Q.

Additionally, while per capita income should lead to a higher growth in rents, as in (4.17), the equation also includes average output per worker (Q/L) as an explanatory variable. These two indicators are almost identical in what it is they explain. The correlation between them is also quite high.

There are a variety of ways of dealing with multicollinearity. The "artificial orthogonalization" of the independent variables data includes versions of principal components analysis and ridge regression. Each of these are statistical methods for transforming the data to reduce the degree of collinearity while retaining most of the essential information. These methods reduce error but introduce bias. Given the difficulties in this data set it is preferred to test for the severity of multicollinearity and caution that when it is severe that empirical results must be interpreted accordingly.

Multicollinearity among the variables explaining the incidence of rents, i.e., those in equation (4.24), can be diagnosed using the Belsley, Kuh and Welsch (BKW) method.[21] dividing the largest eigen value of the **X'X** regression matrix by the smallest eigen value. If the result is larger than 30 then harmful multicollinearity is indicated. See Belsley (1970) and Kmenta (1986) pp. 438-440. The value for equation (4.24)*, without the BWA dummy variable, only comes to 12. Thus, multicollinearity cannot be seen as so severe as to shed doubt on the usefulness of the estimations.

Estimations. Table 4.1 presents the results of the Hausman test described above. The conclusion arrived at here is that investment is not endogenously determined and therefore there is no errors in measurement problem that needs to be addressed through TSLS or the use of instrumental variables.

Equation (4.17)* was estimated using NLS. The results are reported in table 4.2 The estimation results of (4.18)* are found in Table (4.3). Equation (4.18)* is very similar to equation (4.17)* but does not include the manipulations that were based on the Bruno (1968) specification, where labor's marginal product is a linear function of its average product, i.e., $MP_l = cAP_l$. Equation (4.25)* represents the manipulation of (4.17)* that allows the use of OLS. Equation (4.25)* estimation results are reported in Table (4.4)

Table (4.5) compares the neo-classical growth model with the addition of the measure of rents (R/Q) and the degree of political pluralism (RD). All the regressions in Table (4.5) were run with the same data samples. These alternative specifications are compared using changes in the adjusted R^2 and the value of the relevant t-scores. Additionally, the variable SHOCK was attached to equations (4.19)* and (4.20)* to account for the effects on growth of non-economic shocks, such as drought or coups d' etat.

Table (4.6) presents the estimation results for equation (4.21)*, which seeks to explain the impact of a number of variables on the social gross rate of return to capital. Table (4.7) presents the estimation results for equation (4.22)*, which seeks to explain the determinants of the rate of investment.

Tables (4.8) and (4.9) present the estimation results of equations (4.23)* and (4.24)*, which seek to partially explain the determinants of rent-seeking. Equation (4.24)* seeks to explain what causes rents to grow; and (4.19) seeks to explain why rents are higher in some countries than in others. Additionally, the case of Botswana (an outlier) is handled in regressions 3 and 4. Botswana data are not included in regression 3 while a dummy variable indicating Botswana is included in regression 4.

There are a number of difficulties with determining the incidence of rents. The measure of rents is based on a limited set of data, has no precedent and is not regularly compiled by statistical experts. On the one hand, it is uncertain as to how well this term is calculated, there is no alternative data series to compare this measure to.

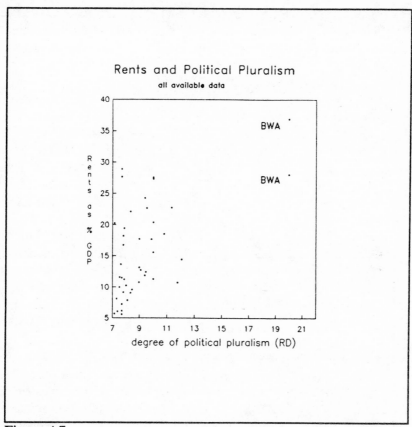

Figure 4.7

Political pluralism in Africa is not well distributed. That is to say, more than two-thirds of African countries fall into Gastil's lowest rankings of rights, while only a few are near the top. There are almost none in the middle. Thus, we cannot be certain as to how much results of some equations are skewed by outliers, in this case Botswana. Chapter 3, discussing figure 3.2, pointed out the sensitivity of the relationship between the degree of political pluralism and economic growth. Figure 4.7 shows the relationship between political pluralism and the incidence of rents for all available data, while figure 4.8 excludes the Botswana data (two observations). It should be clear to the reader that excluding Botswana seems to weaken the apparent relationship between these two variables. For these reasons the regressions in the following tables include a dummy variable for Botswana data.

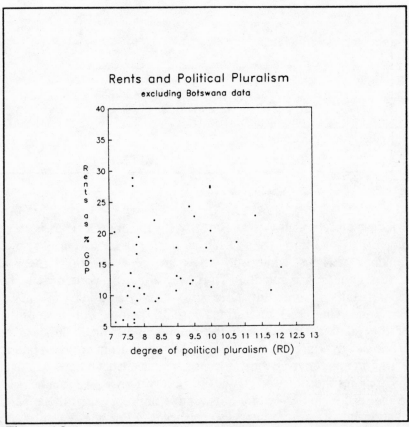

Figure 4.8

Table 4.1: Hausman Test for Endogeneity of the Investment Term:
This test is in two stages: the first estimates the investment/change in
labor function, generating predicted values for use in the second stage.
These are included in estimating equation (4.22)*, where ϵ represents
the predicted values of $\Delta K/\Delta L$.

Data cover African countries in two time periods, 1975-81 and 1981-
85, with one observation per time period.

First Stage: Estimating the Modified Investment Function: OLS

$\Delta K/\Delta L=$	-.57	+.41HOM	+.002G/ΔL	+.05R/ΔL
	$(-1.79)^2$	$(1.47)^1$	(0.11)	(0.18)
	+.053SK	+21.64Q/ΔL	+0.04RD	
	(1.18)	$(6.94)^4$	$(1.33)^1$	
	1.03NIH/ΔL	-15.36TT	-.45TIME	
	$(1.81)^2$	$(-2.58)^4$	$(-3.10)^4$	

$R^2 = .91$ adj. $R^2 = .87$ F-stat. 25.06^4 d.f. 22

Second Stage: Including the Residual (ϵ) Term from the First Stage
into Estimating Equation (4.17a) Using OLS:

$\Delta U=$	-.007	-.728Q/L	+.51RD*Q/L
	(-.43)	$(-1.69)^1$	$(1.34)^1$
+.88NIH/ΔL	+.69ΔK/ΔL	-.04RD*ΔK/ΔL	-.95ϵ
$(1.44)^1$	$(1.59)^1$	(-.86)	(-.65)
	.09rd*ϵ	-.01G/ΔL	.0003PCY
	(0.60)	(-.02)	(0.73)

$R^2 = .76$ adj. $R^2 = .66$ F-stat. 7.18^4 d.f. 20

t-statistics in parentheses single tail t- and F-tests.
[1] significant at the 10% level, [2] 5%, [3] 2.5%, [4] at 1% level.

Table 4.2: General Model: Bruno Specification: NLS:
This table presents estimates of the main empirical equation.
BWA is a dummy variable for Botswana. The estimated equation:

$$\Delta U/\Delta L = f + \beta(1-\Phi RD)Q/L + MR_k(1-\Phi RD)\Delta K/\Delta L$$
$$+ \gamma\Delta G/\Delta L + \epsilon NIH/\Delta L + \phi PCY + v \qquad (4.17)^*$$

| parameter | Dependent variable is $\Delta U/Q$ | | |
	unrestricted	restricted	3
f	-0.02	-0.11	-0.20
	(-0.15	(-0.72)	(-1.40)
β	-4.34	-6.44	-0.22
	$(-1.57)^1$	$(2.38)^3$	(-0.07)
Φ on labor	0.15	0.14	0.17
	$(3.60)^4$	$(4.54)^4$	(0.20)
MR_k	0.36	0.42	0.82
	$(1.40)^1$	$(1.52)^1$	$(2.93)^4$
Φ on capital	0.07	same Φ as L	0.18
	(0.91)		$(7.42)^4$
γ	-0.06	0.12	.52
	(-0.19)	0.39	$(1.55)^1$
ϵ	1.06	1.17	.21
	$(2.02)^2$	$(2.12)^3$	$(0.38)^2$
ϕ	.0001	.0006	.0003
	(0.33)	$(2.35)^3$	(0.91)
BWA			3.08
			$(2.91)^4$
R^2	.72	.68	.79
adjusted R^2	.65	.51	.72
degrees of freedom	28	29	27
F-statistic	10.20^4	10.05^4	12.36^4

t-statistics in parentheses single tail t- and F-tests.
[1] significant at the 10% level, [2] 5%, [3] 2.5%, [4] at 1% level.

Table 4.3: Estimating the General Model Alternative to the Bruno Specification: Using Non-Linear Least Squares:
These estimations are similar to those in table 4.2, but here growth in rents and output is in relation to the level of GDP instead of growth in labor (i.e., the specification is $\Delta U/Q$ instead of $\Delta U/\Delta L$). (4.17)* and (4.18)* cannot be directly compared since they have different independent variables. The estimated equation:

$$\Delta U/Q = \alpha + MR_l(1\text{-}\Phi RD)\Delta L/Q + MR_k(1\text{-}\Phi RD)\Delta K/Q$$
$$+ \gamma\Delta G/Q + \epsilon\Delta NIH/Q + \phi PCY + u \qquad (4.18)*$$

| | Dependent variable is $\Delta U/Q$ | | |
	unrestricted	restricted	3
α	-1.86	-2.67	-2.27
	(-0.54)	(-0.80)	(-0.70)
MR_l	-0.22	-0.02	-.44
	(-1.06)	(-0.28)	$(-1.90)^2$
Φ on labor	0.27	0.90	0.25
	$(4.81)^4$	(0.36)	$(10.14)^4$
MR_k	0.04	-0.04	.50
	(0.23)	(-0.33)	$(1.96)^2$
Φ on capital	-0.55	same Φ as labor	0.17
	(-0.19)		$(4.43)^4$
γ	0.50	0.57	0.63
	$(1.43)^1$	$(1.68)^1$	$(1.88)^2$
ϵ	3.52	3.20	3.21
	$(2.24)^3$	$(2.08)^3$	$(2.16)^3$
ϕ	.001	.002	0.001
	(0.28)	(0.59)	(0.35)
BWA			17.72
			$(2.15)^3$
R^2	.62	.61	.68
adjusted R^2	.53	.53	.58
degrees of freedom	28	29	27
F-statistic	6.63^4	7.55^4	7.13^4

t-statistics in parentheses single tail t- and F-tests.
[1] significant at the 10% level, [2] 5%, [3] 2.5%, [4] at 1% level.

Table 4.4: The General Model Adapted for Using OLS:
This table presents the estimations of equation (4.25)*, which is a manipulation of equation (4.17)* which allows the use of OLS instead of NLS but which is essentially the same. The estimated equation:
$$\Delta U/\Delta L = f + \beta Q/L - \beta\Phi R^*\Delta Q/L + MR_k\Delta K/\Delta L + MR_k\Phi RD^*\Delta K/\Delta L + \gamma\Delta G/\Delta L + \epsilon NIH/\Delta L + v \qquad (4.25)^*$$

Variable	Dependent variable is $\Delta U/\Delta L$	
	1	2
constant	-0.02	-0.20
	(-0.16)	(-1.40)[1]
Q/L	-8.70	-0.42
	(-1.57)[1]	(-0.07)
RD*Q/L	0.34	0.02
	(1.43)[1]	(0.07)
ΔK/L	0.46	0.80
	(1.40)[1]	(2.93)[4]
RD*ΔK/L	-0.01	-0.07
	(-0.57)	(2.52)[4]
ΔG/L	-0.06	0.52
	(-0.19)	(1.55)[1]
NIH/L	1.06	0.21
	(2.02)[2]	(0.37)
PCY	0.0001	0.0003
	(0.33)	(0.91)
BWA		3.08
		(2.91)[4]
R^2	.72	.79
adj. R^2	.65	.72
d.f.	28	27
F-statistic	10.20[4]	12.36[4]

t-statistics in parentheses single tail t- and F-tests.
[1] significant at the 10% level, [2] 5%, [3] 2.5%, [4] at 1% level.

Table 4.5: Comparing the Rent-Augmented Growth Model to the Neo- Classical Growth Model: OLS

This table allows assessment of the effect of the size of rents within the neo-classical growth model. Estimating equations:

$$\Delta Q/Q = \delta_0 + \delta_1 \Delta L/Q + \delta_2 \Delta K/Q + \delta_3 G/Q + \delta_4 RD$$
$$+ \delta_5 NIH/Q + \delta_6 SHOCK + u \qquad (4.19)*$$
$$\Delta Q/Q = \alpha_0 + \alpha_1 L/Q + \alpha_2 \Delta K/Q + \alpha_3 G/Q + \alpha_4 RD$$
$$+ \delta_5 NIH/Q + \delta_6 SHOCK + \alpha_7 R/Q + e \qquad (4.20)*$$

Variable	Dependent variable is $\Delta Q/Q$			
	1	2	3	4
constant	-3.14	2.59	-3.75	1.97
(t-stat)	(-1.10)	(0.54)	(-1.30)	(0.40)
$\Delta L/Q$	0.03	0.02	0.03	0.02
	(0.80)	(0.57)	(0.76)	(0.53)
$\Delta K/Q$	0.17	0.14	0.13	0.10
	(1.53)[1]	(1.24)	(1.08)	(0.80)
G/Q	-0.08	-0.05	0.006	0.03
	(-0.92)	(-0.60)	(0.05)	(0.29)
RD	0.48	-0.14	0.68	0.07
	(2.06)[3]	(-0.29)	(2.32)[3]	(0.14)
NIH/Q	2.00	1.73	1.95	1.69
	(1.45)[1]	(1.26)	(1.42)[1]	(1.24)
SHOCK	-0.50	-0.63	-0.55	-0.68
	(-1.33)[1]	(-1.65)[1]	(-1.44)[1]	(-1.76)[2]
R/Q		-0.17	-0.17	
		(-1.13)	(-1.14)	
BWA		8.39		8.36
		(1.46)[1]		(1.46)[1]
R^2	.43	.47	.45	.49
adjusted R^2	.32	.34	.32	.35
d.f.	30	29	29	28
F-statistic	3.76	3.65	3.43	3.39

t-statistics in parentheses single tail t- and F-tests.
[1] significant at the 10% level, [2] 5%, [3] 2.5%, [4] at 1% level.

Table 4.6: Determinants of the Gross Social Rate of Return to Capital: Using OLS:
The estimations in this table seek to explain the impact of a number of variables on the gross social rate of return to capital. Among other things, the share of rents in GDP (R/Q) is included as one of the determinants of the gross social rate of return. Estimating equation:

$$\text{RETURN} = r_0 + r_1 \text{HOM} + r_2 \text{R/Q} + r_3 \text{G/Q} + r_4 \text{SHOCK}$$
$$+ r_5 \text{Q/L} + r_6 \text{RD} + r_7 \text{NIH/Q} + \gamma \qquad (4.21)*$$

Variable	Dependent variable is RETURN		
	1	2	3
Constant	0.24	0.24	0.49
	$(2.05)^2$	$(2.10)^3$	$(2.22)^2$
HOM	-0.02	--	-0.03
	(-0.14)		(0.21)
R/Q	-0.001	-0.001	0.0007
	(-0.11)	(-0.10)	(0.09)
G/Q	-0.006	-0.007	-0.006
	$(-1.48)^1$	$(-1.55)^1$	(-1.45)
SHOCK	-0.006	-0.006	-0.006
	(-0.33)	(-0.34)	(-0.33)
Q/L	-0.52	-.50	-0.40
	(-1.22)	(-1.29)	(-0.93)
RD	0.02	0.02	-0.008
	$(1.62)^1$	$(1.72)^2$	(-0.29)
NIH/Q	0.09	0.08	0.07
	$(1.32)^1$	$(1.35)^1$	(1.02)
BWA		0.38	
		$(1.32)^1$	
R^2	.31	.30	.36
adjusted R^2	.08	.12	.11
d.f.	22	23	21
F-statistic	1.38	1.68	1.47

t-statistics in parentheses single tail t- and F-tests.
[1] significant at the 10% level, [2] 5%, [3] 2.5%, [4] at 1% level.

Table 4.7: Determinants of the Investment Rate: Using OLS:
These estimations indicate the determinants, including rents-to-GDP
(R/Q), of investment. Estimating equation:

$$\Delta K/Q = i_0 + i_1 HOM + i_2 R/Q + i_3 G/Q + i_4 SHOCK + i_5 Q/L +$$
$$+ i_6 RD + i_7 NIH/Q + i_8 TT + i_9 TIME + \alpha \qquad (4.22)*$$

Variable	Dependent variable is $\Delta K/Q$			
	1	2	3	4
Constant	2.88	2.93	2.72	7.93
	(0.92)	(0.95)	(0.89)	$(1.43)^1$
HOM	1.87	0.56	--	1.52
	(0.54)	(0.19)		(0.44)
R/Q	-0.47	-0.48	-0.47	-0.48
	$(-2.40)^3$	$(-2.32)^3$	$(-2.46)^3$	$(-2.46)^3$
G/Q	0.64	0.63	0.64	0.66
	$(5.63)^4$	$(5.66)^4$	$(5.88)^4$	$(5.76)^4$
SHOCK	-0.12	-0.20	-0.12	-0.16
	(-0.21)	(-0.39)	(-0.22)	(-0.30)
Q/L	9.18	--	5.72	11.76
	(0.74)		(0.54)	(0.93)
RD	0.75	0.87	0.84	0.12
	$(1.87)^2$	$(2.37)^3$	$(2.30)^3$	(0.17)
NIH/Q	0.96	1.29	1.02	0.38
	(0.54)	(0.76)	(0.58)	(0.20)
TT	-130.54	-121.96	-122.76	-103.50
	$(-1.66)^1$	$(-1.59)^1$	$(-1.62)^1$	(-1.23)
TIME	-6.12	-5.75	-6.02	-6.15
	$(-3.40)^4$	$(-3.36)^4$	$(-3.41)^4$	$(3.43)^4$
BWA				8.33
				(1.09)
R^2	.82	.82	.82	.83
adjusted R^2	.75	.76	.76	.75
d.f.	22	23	23	21
F-statistic	11.33^4	12.94^4	13.12^4	10.41^4

t-statistics in parentheses single tail t- and F-tests.
[1] significant at the 10% level, [2] 5%, [3] 2.5%, [4] at 1% level.

Table 4.8: Determinants of the Growth in Rents: Using OLS:
The estimates in table 4.8 indicate the variables that are expected to
affect the growth in rents. Among these are investment ($\Delta K/Q$), the
size of government (G/Q), the degree of political pluralism (RD),
social homogeneity (HOM), the level of per capita income (PCY) and
the size of rents relative to GDP (R/Q). Estimating equation:

$$\Delta R/Q = \pi_0 + \pi_1 \Delta K/Q + \pi_2 G/Q + \pi_3 RD + \pi_4 HOM$$
$$+ \pi_5 PCY + \pi_6 R/Q + \tau \qquad (4.23)*$$

Variable	Dependent variable is $\Delta R/Q$			
	1	2	3	4
constant	-2.94	-2.80	-2.96	-2.64
	$(-3.56)^4$	$(-3.47)^4$	(-0.78)	$(-1.69)^2$
$\Delta K/Q$	0.04	0.04	0.05	0.03
	(0.63)	(0.64)	(0.78)	(0.53)
G/Q	0.06	0.05	0.06	0.06
	$(1.98)^2$	$(1.81)^2$	$(2.31)^3$	$(1.96)^2$
RD	0.10	0.05	0.11	0.07
	(0.86)	(0.50)	(0.97)	(0.53)
HOM	0.62	0.79	--	0.61
	(0.67)	(0.86)		(0.64)
PCY	-0.001	--	-.001	-0.0009
	(-0.86)		(-1.02)	(0.76)
R/Q	0.09	0.09	0.09	0.09
	$(2.13)^3$	$(2.03)^3$	$(2.11)^3$	$(2.07)^2$
BWA				0.52
				(0.23)
R^2	.54	.54	.54	.55
adjusted R^2	.46	.47	.47	.45
d.f.	33	34	34	32
F-statistic	6.64^4	7.88^4	8.00^4	5.53^4

t-statistics in parentheses single tail t- and F-tests.
[1] significant at the 10% level, [2] 5%, [3] 2.5%, [4] at 1% level.

Table 4.9: Determinants of the Size of Rents: Using OLS:
This table addresses the incidence of rents. Rents are expected to be greater relative to GDP (i.e., R/Q) where the size of government and the per capita incomes are greater, and less where there is greater political pluralism and social homogeneity.
Estimating equation:
$$R/Q = f_0 + f_1 G/Q + f_2 PCY + f_3 RD + f_4 HOM + \phi \qquad (4.24)^*$$

Variable	Dependent variable is R/Q			
	1	2	3	4
constant	-3.06	1.03	-0.097	2.87
	(-0.99)	(0.44)	(-0.16)	(1.15)
G/Q	0.34	0.34	0.34	0.34
	$(3.52)^4$	$(3.32)^4$	$(3.48)^4$	$(3.48)^4$
PCY	0.004	0.009	0.004	0.006
	(0.82)	$(2.42)^3$	(0.88)	$(1.42)^1$
RD	0.80	--	0.54	--
	$(1.98)^1$		(0.70)	
HOM	-1.46	0.23	-1.62	-1.54
	(-0.41)	(0.06)	(-0.45)	(0.43)
BWA	--	--	3.42	8.48
			(0.40)	$(1.88)^2$
R^2	.59	.54	.59	.58
adjusted R^2	.54	.51	.53	.54
d.f.	36	37	35	36
F-statistic	12.84^4	17.45^4	10.06^4	12.64^4

t-statistics in parentheses single tail t- and F-tests.
[1] significant at the 10% level, [2] 5%, [3] 2.5%, [4] at 1% level.

Interpretation and Summary

Interpretation of these results must be tempered by an appreciation of the data problems and the fact that several of the indicators reflect conceptualizations that have not had wide currency among the economics profession and about which the statistical properties are not well investigated. The manipulated Gastil index and the Gastil index itself show very little variance since about two-thirds of African countries fall into the two lowest categories of civil liberties while only a few are at the top end of the scale. The measures of rents have not been used elsewhere and there is no precedent for their use. Additionally, several sources of rents have not been included, especially import quotas. Even labor force figures are guesses by experts and are not based on employment surveys. Nonetheless, a number of interesting results arise from these tables.

Table 4.1 tests for endogeneity of investment in the general model. The coefficient of the term e, which represents the possible degree of error in measurement (in this case, from the possibility that investment is endogenously determined), is not significantly different from zero, implying that error will not significantly enter into this specification through this variable so as to violate the basic assumptions of BLUE for OLS. I conclude that OLS and NLS, where appropriate, would yield the best linear (non-linear) unbiased estimates (BLUE).

Tables 4.2, 4.3, and 4.4 deal with the general rent-augmented growth model. The F-statistics indicate that these various estimations and that these regressors explain a significant degree of the variance in the dependent variable, $\Delta U/Q$. Botswana is treated as a possible outlier throughout these tables and a dummy variable (BWA) is used to indicate the presence of Botswana data. In most instances including BWA in the regressions raises the regressions R^2 and the coefficient of BWA is significant. In only some instances does adding the BWA dummy variable cause changes in other estimated parameters.

The sign of Φ in tables 4.2 and 4.3 is as predicted by theory, except in table 4.3 where in the unrestricted (the restricted regression holds Φ constant for both labor and capital) regression Φ on capital was negative but not significant. However, when the BWA indicator was included in the regression Φ became positive and significant. The Φ, being positive, is consistent with the notion of institutional costs of rent-seeking.

The Φ on labor is significantly greater than zero but the Φ on capital is not significantly greater than zero except when the BWA is included. When the NLS estimations are restricted to generate only one Φ for both labor and capital, Φ remained significantly positive. In table 4.2 the restriction reduced the R^2. The drop came about due to the fact that there is one less regressor since the significance of all the other variables, as well as that of Φ, increased with the restriction. Even without the restriction, from table 4.2 regression one we see that the Φ on capital of .07 with a standard error of about .08, is not significantly less than .15, the Φ on labor. When the restriction is placed on the alternative to Bruno specification of table 4.3 the overall goodness of fit improves slightly, in terms of the F-statistic, but this occurs solely due to the increase in degree of freedom rather than from improvements in the significance of any of the coefficients, indeed, Φ becomes entirely insignificant while the coefficient for net investment in human capital declines and the MR_k turns negative, although it is insignificant.

The β of table 4.2 is negative and significant, as expected, indicating an inverse relationship between the average product of labor, which can serve as an indicator of the capital-labor ratio, and the total marginal potential output of labor ($\Delta U / \Delta L$). This provides some support to convergence. However, when the estimation includes BWA the β becomes insignificant, and so throws doubt on convergence.

The estimates of the marginal rent of capital (MR_k) in table 4.2 are consistent with marginal products of capital found in other works, that is, the marginal rents found here are somewhat larger than the marginal products in Kormendi and Meguire (1985), Barro (1989a&b) and Easterly and Wetzel (1989), and those of table 4.5, and these estimates are significant at the ten percent level of confidence. However, in the BWA regression the MR_k is larger still. The MR_ks in the first and second estimations of table 4.3 are much smaller than expected, and they are not significant. However, when the BWA indicator is included the MR_k rises to be consistent with estimates elsewhere and also becomes significant.

The coefficients on government growth in the first two estimations of tables 4.2 are neither significant nor surprising. The results of this variable have been mixed in several other empirical investigations into economic growth, such as Grier and Tullock (1989), and are consistent with Easterly and Wetzel's (1989) attempts to reconcile the contradictory impacts of government growth. Additionally, the theory of rent-seeking leads one to expect that growing government would encourage or facilitate greater rent-seeking, hence the relationship could encourage rent-seeking but also contraction of productive activities. Yet, in the third regression, when BWA is included, the government coefficient becomes both positive and significant.

The coefficients on net investment in human capital in tables 4.2, 4.3, 4.4, and 4.5 are positive, as expected, although the significance declines or disappears when BWA is included. These results provide further empirical support for human capital theories of growth.

The coefficient ϕ on per capita income is similarly ambiguous as that on government spending. Per capita income and output per laborer are highly correlated and it therefore makes little sense to try to explain the significance of this variable. The variable was mainly kept in the regression since the level of per capita income should positively affect the growth in rents. Due to the conflicting nature of this variable no significant impact can be found.

The temptation to compare the rent-augmented and neo-classical models is compelling. However, it is impossible to directly compare the regression results since each has a different dependent variable. Instead, in table 4.5 the neo-classical model with and without the measure of rents (R/Q) is estimated. By adding R/Q to the neo-classical model little overall explanatory value is added, in terms of the adjusted R^2. When the neo-classical model including BWA is estimated adding R/Q adds very little (the adjusted R^2 increases from .34 to .35) explanatory power.

In two of the estimates of table 4.5 net investment in human capital is shown to contribute to growth. When BWA is included the NIH coefficient becomes insignificant, although its size does not change. Also, physical capital investment ($\Delta K/Q$) contributes to growth, as expected, and the coefficients are consistent with those in table 4.2. The contribution of labor force growth to GDP growth is not shown to be statistically significant in any of the regressions. This may be because labor forces have continued to grow throughout each of the countries studied during these two period yet economic growth has been slow in most cases: and, in many cases per capita GDP has been on the decline while in others total GDP has been declining. IN practice, it is difficult to get a positive coefficient when the dependent variable is declining and the independent variable is increasing. This indicates that this study is perhaps not a study of economic growth so much as it is a study of economic decline.

In each case, the impact of political pluralism on economic growth, whether as an indicator of property rights as suggested by Barro (1989a&b) and Grier and Tullock (1989) or as an indicator of the degree of institutional competition for rents, is positive.

The dependent variable in table 4.6, although labelled RETURN, is actually the inverse of the familiar ICOR. AS a rate of return it assumes that all returns are to capital. It also should be seen as the rate of social return, because it does not include the purely private returns of rent-seeking.[22] In no instance can the regressions of table 4.6 be considered good fits. Yet, except for HOM (homogeneity), all coefficients are of the expected signs. And, the impact of the degree of political pluralism seems to be significantly positive, as does the impact of net investment in human capital. This might be interpreted as showing that when there is greater political pluralism there is less diversion of resources into non-productive activities. That NIH seems to raise the returns to capital is somewhat supportive of Lucas' (1987) hypothesis that investment in human capital has the external benefit of raising the productivity of all factors (or at least raising the productivity of factors other than just labor). Although NIH's coefficient is positive, it is not significant.

Table 4.7 presents the estimation results of equation (4.17a) which estimates the investment function. Each estimation is shown by the F-test to explain a significant degree of the variance in the investment ratio. HOM has a positive, though not significant, coefficient, which is consistent with expectations. The level of rents is negatively and significantly related to the investment rate. The size of government is positively and significantly related to the investment rate. Considering the positive relationship between (R/Q) and (G/Q) it is surprising to get significant and opposite results for these two variables: this indicates the strength of these two variables in determining the rate of investment. Net investment in human capital has a positive but insignificant coefficient. The time variable is negative and significant, which is consistent with the notion that the drying up of international liquidity in the 1980s severely reduced the available resources for investment in African countries.

The oddest result is the apparent negative relationship between the improvement in the international terms of trade and investment. One would have expected that improving terms of trade might attract investment, especially to the export sector, yet the reverse appears true. This seeming paradox can possibly be explained as follows: Investment includes both private and public sector capital expenditures, without a breakdown between the two. Given the development paradigms most African countries have been following[23] a major share of all investment is from the public sector. For those countries where the terms of trade have deteriorated most sharply there have been avenues for getting more foreign grants and concessional lending.[24] These foreign grants and concessional loans often are tied to particular development (capital) expenditures and usually do not fund current spending. Thus, deteriorating terms of trade may trigger cheaper foreign money, which in turn may offset declining private investment. The data to disentangle this paradox are not systematically compiled, but this would make an interesting research topic.

Tables 4.8 and 4.9 address the incidence of rents. 4.8 addresses the growth in rents, while 4.9 addresses the determinants of rent size relative to the economy (R/Q). From table 4.8 the clearest answers seem to be that rents grow most where rents are already largest[25] and where government is large. It is surprising to not find a stronger relationship between economic growth and growth in rents, but this may arise because of simultaneity problems, since reduced rent-seeking frees resources for greater productive uses.

It was expected that the coefficient of RD would be negative, instead it is positive but insignificant. This may be due to the positive relationship between RD and economic growth. It was also expected that the sign of HOM would be negative, since a more homogenous society might find it more difficult to organize into effective rent-seeking interest groups. Instead, its coefficient is positive but insignificant. In the second regression per capita income (PCY) is excluded since its previously estimated coefficient was not significant, homogeneity (HOM) was dropped from the third regression for the same reason. Neither dropping PCY not HOM made any significant changes in the estimation results; other coefficients and the R^2 changed little. Similarly, including BWA made little difference.

Table 4.9 presents the estimations of equation (4.19), which seeks to explain the incidence of rents, in terms of the size of rents relative to the economy (G/Q). Rents are clearly positively associated with the size of government, as expected. There is also evidence from regressions 2 and 4 that rents are positively related to per capita income, again as expected. However, regression 1 indicates a positive relationship between the degree of political pluralism and rent size, which becomes insignificant when BWA is included. Keeping in mind that political pluralism and per capita incomes are fairly highly correlated[26] when RD is excluded, as in the second regression, the coefficient for PCY becomes positive.

In sum, the estimations presented here provide considerable support for the hypotheses of chapter 3 and tend to confirm many aspects of the rent-augmented growth model developed in this chapter.

Notes

1. The question arises, if there is no output can there still be rents? The answer is, yes. Rents need not only include transfers of income but can also include transfers of wealth or resources. For instance, taking slaves is seeking rent.

2. c does not represent total resource costs of rent-seeking. Instead, it refers only to those costs facing rent-seekers arising from institutional competition for rents, as described in chapter 3.

3. This formulation refers only to the decision facing individuals or institutions. It cannot hold in the aggregate since all distributions are from Q only. However, at the microeconomic level this formulation is a valid representation of the choices available between rent-seeking or producing goods and services.

4. This is already in violation of the notion that rents tend to grow more rapidly than output of goods and services.

5. This is somewhat parallel to L' Hopital's rule, which is: the limit of the ratio of two functions, if it exists, equals the ratio of the derivatives of those functions, respectively.

6. Euler's theorem says that when production functions are linear, homogenous the sum of the marginal products (and in this case, marginal rents) of each factor (in this case, productively and non-productively used capital) times the level and use of that factor adds up to the total output (and rents).

7. The gross rate of return infers all returns to capital while all other factors are assumed to not contribute to output and are free factors. This term has been used elsewhere, e.g., Agarwala (1983) and Anderson (1987).

8. See World Bank (1989c).

9. Neo-classical theory and diminishing returns to variables holds that where capital-labor ratios are low, such as in Africa compared to the rest of the world, returns to capital ought to be high.

10. See chapter 1 to revisit the discussion on the major policy issues in Africa.

11. Reid (1970) illustrated the "power of a minimal amount of data employed within a consistent framework and simple model to get around a seemingly 'missing' datum" in attempting to estimate the costs of trade distortions imposed upon the American colonies under the Navigation Acts.

12. This is consistent with Posner's (1975) findings, as discussed in chapter 2, that dead-weight losses from monopoly in American industry were only 3 percent of the rent-seeking losses.

13. A numerical example from Botswana: In 1984 total tariff revenues in constant 1980 dollars were $175 million. Total imports were $642 million. Dividing 175 by 642 yields an effective tariff rate (t) of 27%. Value-added of the manufacturing sector in Botswana in 1984 totaled $373 million. 27% of $373 million is $101 million, which is how the rent transferred to domestic manufacturers was calculated.

14. See Jaeger and Humphreys (1988).

15. This will not significantly affect empirical testing of the model. Total rents were aggregated two ways: R1 includes all the rent calculations; R2 excludes rents from the non-market allocation of capital. The correlation between R1 and R2 as ratios to GDP (i.e., R1/Q and R2/Q) is almost 100%, see table A.2.2 in the data Appendix. For the empirical testing in this chapter only R1 was used since it contains the most information.

16. Investment data are not available for public and private investment expenditure separately.

17. See Morrison, Mitchell, and Paden (1989) and Berry (1970).

18. Although different sources indicate different numbers of languages in the same country at the same time, the differences are small and do not generally alter rankings.

19. NLS, a maximum likelihood estimation, is an iterative process, calculating estimates of approximate derivatives with respect to each parameter. Small changes in the parameters are proposed and then the dependent variable is regressed on them. This regression generates a vector of proposed changes in the parameters, which in turn are again used in the next iterative regression. The process continues as long as each iteration reduces the regression's sum of squared residuals. If NLS is used on a linear equation the resulting estimated parameters will be identical to those generated by OLS.

20. See Kmenta (1986) pp. 365-66 for a discussion of how the Hausman test for specification error can be applied in instances of possible simultaneity.

21. The test involves dividing the largest eigen value of the $X'X$ regression matrix by the smallest eigen value. If the result is larger than 30 then harmful multicollinearity is indicated.

22. See figure 4.2 and the discussion of errors in variables.

23. See chapter 1.

24. For instance, the IDA-eligible countries experienced the sharpest deteriorations in their terms of trade but were eligible for a special program of increased donor support. For a discussion see World Bank/UNDP (1989).

25. This does not imply that the growth rate of rents is associated with rent size.

26. The coefficient of correlation is 70 percent.

5

Conclusions and Implications

This chapter presents general conclusions, discusses areas for future research and points out some policy implications.

Conclusions

The objective of this project has been to improve our understanding of the determinants of economic growth in Africa. The approach taken was to meld neo-classical growth theory with an extension of the theory of competitive rent-seeking. Neo-classical growth models assume that all factors are optimally allocated to productive uses. The rent-augmented model assumes that factors are allocated between productive and non-productive uses. By including rent-seeking into models of growth factor use has been better accounted for.

Five sources of rents were calculated: tariff revenues, protection to domestic manufacturers, monopsonistic behavior of agricultural marketing boards, and non-market allocation of foreign exchange and investment funds. Rents are a very large share of GDP in some African countries. These estimates range from 6-37% of GDP, with the lowest being the very poor, small government, Niger and the highest being the moderate income, very large government, but slightly more democratic Lesotho. The calculations of these rents played an integral part of the analysis but are very crude and subject to mismeasurement.

Rent-seeking slows growth in two ways. First, in that rent-seeking represents a diversion of resources from productive to unproductive uses less of a nation's investment and labor growth is applied toward increasing output of real goods and services. Second, economic rents are transfers of income or of wealth and as such represent a tax on the means of production. In this sense rents lower the incentives to invest or to work since rents reduce the net returns to all factors. With weakened incentives we should expect less investment and less economic growth.

The degree of political pluralism has been found to play an important role in rent-seeking and economic growth. Under democratic regimes the fruits of rent-seeking are less secure and the costs faced by rent-seekers are higher. This provides some disincentive to rent-seeking.

A number of important aspects of rent-seeking have been demonstrated. Rents as a share of GDP tend to be positively related to per capita income and government size. The theoretical chapter also leads us to expect that there would be more rent-seeking under less democratic regimes, but this has not been confirmed. There is considerable interaction among per capita incomes, government size and the degree of political pluralism, which complicates the statistical analysis and makes it difficult or impossible to sort out the different contributions of these factors to rent-seeking.

The role of government in Africa's development is mixed. There is a strongly negative relationship between the size of government and the rate of economic growth. Additionally, it has been shown that government size and rent-seeking are directly related. Yet, it has also been shown that government education spending and other investment spending are important sources of growth. The challenge to Africa is to increase the efficiency of government spending, reduce the rent-seeking waste associated with government spending while at the same time retaining the important human and reproducible capital spending.

Shocks, man-made and natural, of course, slow growth, particularly through the impact on investment. Drought, coups d' etat, and urban riots tend to reduce investor confidence. Lower investment results in slower growth. Shocks also appear to be associated with rent-seeking.

Although this has not been well developed, it is understandable. Where rent-seeking is rampant we should expect social and political upheaval as various members of society vie for large, not widely distributed rents, and the reins of government as the source of those rents. The empirical results are not strong enough to draw strong conclusions in which we can have confidence. Nonetheless, if rent-seeking does give rise to political and civil disturbances, thereby harming investor confidence, then this is yet another channel through which rent-seeking slows growth.

It is hoped that this book has made some contribution to the theories of rent-seeking, economic growth, and, to a lesser extent, the government's role in the development process. Nonetheless, there is much more to be done.

The study made no attempt to investigate the distribution of product in these countries. While factors are used to produce both output and rents, only output can actually be distributed. Who gets these rents and what attributes do successful rent-seekers possess? Are rent-seekers particularly astute, amoral, prone to law breaking, politically sensitive? Do ethnic and social mores play a role in rent-seeking and what empirical evidence is there to support this notion. If rents are taken from the fruit of productive activities how do non-rent-seekers perceive the fairness of the economic system and how would such feelings affect their decision making? What links are there between rent-seeking and violence and political instability.

Data problems in Africa are severe. This analysis has been very data intense. This has limited the number of countries that could be included in the major statistical tests. Mauritius, one of the most democratic countries of Africa, if not the most democratic, was not included. Mozambique, a country under anarchy, was also excluded for lack of data. Including Ethiopia would have rounded out the analysis and would have incorporated the second-most populated African country into the study. Even for the countries that were included, the data problems were usually severe. The treatment of missing data has been on an <u>ad hoc</u> basis. More systematic treatment might ensure more reliable, credible results, but would have resulted in only two or three countries being included in the study.

The degree of democracy is an important indicator in the study. But, its measurement is inadequate. There is insufficient distinction among countries in terms of one democratic country being much more democratic than another, or the degree of oppression among the non-democratic countries. Improvements in this indicator are necessary to take the analysis much further. The problem, however, goes beyond improvement in the indicator. Indeed, a more developed theory of the state along the lines implied in this book -- where the state is seen as an arena where rents are extracted and distributed according to institutional competition and the distribution of power in the political process -- is necessary to improve our understanding of how institutional arrangements interact and encourage rent-seeking.

This research shows the impacts of the degree of political pluralism on rent-seeking, investment and growth, and leads to the conclusion that greater political pluralism would be socially beneficial. Still, there is a great need to investigate the dynamics of changing the political system. As a country changes its political system, from, say, the one party state to a free and open, multi-party elective system, what will happen to economic and civil stability, investment, rent-seeking, and economic growth as the country proceeds through these changes? This question has not been answered in this book. The answer, however, is of great importance to a number of African countries (e.g., Cote d' Ivoire and Zambia) that are slowly testing the democratic waters. Answers to this question would also be helpful in designing future foreign aid and policy reform programs.

Understanding the relationships between the government sector and economic and social variables needs to be improved upon. Such studies could be single country studies, comparative country studies, or cross-sectional studies. More important than understanding the "demand" for government services is to sort out the benefits and costs of government behavior for economic performance and social welfare. This is an old saw, but empirical growth models that include the government sector as a structural variable seem to tell only a very limited side of the story.

Empirical investigations into the nature of the rent-seeking society might include links between economic structure (such as the degree of manufacturing in society) and the prevalence of rent-seeking. A country's trade structure may be related to the prevalence of rent-seeking. For instance, mono-exporters may perceive fewer opportunities for productive resource use and may rely upon royalties. Countries that import a great deal, especially those with few ports of entry, may find imposing and collecting tariffs so easy as to make this a convenient source of rents to government, smugglers, and domestic producers alike.

Cross-country studies should incorporate other regions. Poor economic performance is almost as great a problem in Latin America as it has been in Africa, and the data are better. Including Asian LDCs would serve to add greater variety to the study and would better test the robustness of the theories and the empirical methods.

There have been a number of cases that do not neatly conform to the theory as expressed here. For instance, in Botswana rents make up a very large share of the economy, yet the country enjoys democracy and the highest growth rates. To explain why Botswana should be treated as an "outlier" and why rents are much larger in that country than the theory leads us to expect requires much more in-depth study of that particular country, and comparison of Botswana with one or two other countries. Country cases would enhance the richness and robustness of this study. Comparative studies could help to better link the types of institutions, rent-seeking and economic performance, by providing much richer detail and explaining anomalous results. To indicate the behavior of a set of state institutions with a value of 20, or 8, or 10, misses much of how these state institutions behave. A comparative study, such as Ekelund and Tollison's study of England and France, for a pair of African countries would be fruitful and more directly applicable for today's development economists.

Policy Implications

To the extent the conclusions drawn in this study are valid, there remain important implications to flesh out. If African economies are stabilized but there is no democratization, can we expect reform programs to be sustainable after external pressures have eased? If rent-seeking behavior adequately explains much of Africa's growth problems, why would we expect African policy makers to actually make real structural adjustments in their economies? If democratic institutions really do improve factor use and raise the growth rate, how do we stimulate the development of such institutions?

Policy recommendations should be directed to the audience and the audience's objectives. For instance, although this book draws the conclusion that democracy is better for economic growth than is dictatorship there is little reason to expect that dictators will be willing to give up their power for the sake of improving growth for the national economy. For countries honestly experimenting with opening up the political process, however, this research lends encouragement and support. More open political processes should generate greater economic growth.

In Chapter 1 it was pointed out that many African leaders have publicly committed themselves to economic reform. These reforms may not be fully implemented and progress in reform implementation varies greatly from country to country.[1] Nonetheless, countries such as Ghana and the Gambia have made great strides in reducing rent generating price distortions and have extended the market process in the allocation of resources. These countries should expect that if their reforms are sustained and confidence in the sincerity of the reform efforts can take hold that growth will be achievable and living standards will rise. In the Gambia the political process is fairly open, with considerable competition among state institutions and a relatively high degree of accountability of the state to the population. Once rents in the Gambia are reduced and a more rapid growth path is achieved there is considerable optimism that rent-seeking in the future can be held in check and that growth can be sustained over the long haul. For Ghana there is less cause for optimism. Although the present leader (Rawlings) seems fully committed to economic reform he has little interest in introducing greater political pluralism at the national level. After a few years of economic growth in Ghana there is a possibility of recidivism, i.e., the country may slip back into rampant rent-seeking and resultant slow growth, either because another leader, less committed to liberal economics may take the reins or because the temptations to Mr. Rawlings and his ruling structure will have become too great to resist.

Implications for the international donor community, based on the assumption that the objective is to generate sustainable economic growth in Africa, will differ somewhat. In a way, the strings attached to foreign assistance and developmental lending with regard to shaping economic policy and managing the allocation of public resources can be seen as an injection of competition into the arena of non-market decision making. Foreign donors often demand that certain policy changes be taken before financial assistance is given to African governments. These demands generally are to open greater segments of these economies to market forces and to reduce the role and size of government. Such demands are inimical to the narrow interests of many important or powerful people and institutions but include financial resources to support and enforce these demands. Some bilateral donors have tied political reforms to economic support. For instance, the U.S. government has reduced assistance to Kenya because of the Kenyan government's restrictions on freedoms. Additionally, the U.S. has provided assistance and monitoring of the broadening of the power base in Liberia's political system in the mid-1980s. Obviously that was not successful. The World Bank, the single largest institution in terms of financial assistance to Africa, by its own charter is unable to consider political conditions on its lending programs.

World Bank structural adjustment lending can only occur if a country is participating in an International Monetary Fund (IMF) stabilization program. Additionally, debt relief from foreign official and non-official sources is almost always predicated upon meeting IMF program conditions. A major condition of IMF lending is the reduction of fiscal deficit, often through the reduction of government spending. The international community needs to concern itself with how African governments meet this conditionality. This book has provided evidence of the positive role human capital investment plays in creating economic growth. Stabilization and structural adjustment programs that ignore the positive impact of government spending on eduction ignore an important source of growth and recovery. In particular, even if such programs can improve intermediate term growth the question of sustainability arises. If human capital has been decimated can we expect long term growth to be achievable even if short term growth has been temporarily won?

International institutions and some bilateral aid donors may put pressure on governments and state institutions in general to undertake economic reforms, but unless there is a real opening up of the political process there is the danger that once international pressures have subsided that these countries will slip back into their old rent-seeking ways.

The constituency groups that form around and are given sustenance by rents may whither and die if international pressures can be maintained long enough to hold rents in check. This is rather wishful thinking. While the international community can help hold rents to a minimum other activities can foster the distribution of power within African societies and raise the degree of institutional competition. Donor assistance conditioned on political liberalization, greater basic human rights and rule of law would go far in this direction. Additionally, donor support to programs that encourage popular participation in non-market decision making, such as strengthening agricultural cooperatives and community development groups, may help to give voice to the otherwise disenfranchised.

Africa's future depends upon the prospects for institutionalizing both liberal economic policies and political freedom.

Notes

1. For an assessment of reform implementation in Africa, see Gallagher (1990/91).

Appendix 1

Data Notes

This appendix discusses the quality of African data in general, the sources of the statistical data used in this book, and the methods used for calculating ratios, growth rates, etc. A matrix of correlations among the variables used in the book is found in table A.1 and table A.2 presents the data actually used in the regressions of chapter 4 and for the various graphs.

Data Quality

Large shares of national income are outside of the monetary economy and as such are either ignored or estimated through a process no better than guessing. In a recent conference of African Planners, Statisticians and Demographers (Joint Conference of African Planners, Statisticians and Demographers, January 1990, Addis Ababa) the United Nations Economic Commission for Africa reported on many of the existing data gaps and short-comings in the statistical systems of African governments. Even the size and rate of growth of population in some countries is uncertain. Consumer price indices are often based on consumption surveys taken in the early 1960s, when incomes, income distribution, goods, and consumption patterns were all quite different from today. Because of high tariffs, quotas and over- valued currencies imports are often under-invoiced while exports

135

are sometimes smuggled out. In the 1980s Liberia's statistical discrepancy in the balance of payments was about 10 percent of monetary GDP, indicating capital outflows that could not be accounted for. Although more Africans are employed in agriculture than in all other sectors combined the volume of agricultural output is rarely well documented. Data on infant mortality are little more than guesses. Sometimes infant mortality rates are derived from very limited samples, often limited to regions of a country where foreign donor assistance in the health sector has been active. Censuses in some countries have not been conducted since the early 1970s. Perhaps the most obvious lack of data is on labor markets. There are no observations of paid wage rates except for the government and formal private and quasi-public sectors. Broad unit labor costs are totally unavailable for Africa. Unemployment is assumed away and low productivity, self-employment and under-employment are assumed in its place. Labor force figures are population estimates multiplied by the portion of the population considered to be "economically active" rather than the results of household employment surveys. There is no breakdown between private and public investment in the national accounts. Chander (1990) accurately describes the situation regarding information systems in most African countries as a severe constraint on prospective growth and development. For many African countries there are almost no reliable social and economic data.

Despite these difficulties the need to undertake analysis of African economies is urgent. Those who are interested in what happens to the poorest of the poor in this world have cast their eyes toward the dark continent. Foreign assistance to Africa is greater on a per capita basis than in any other continent. For Africa's sake the need to undertake research is paramount. The difficulties entailed in undertaking that research are insufficient reason for avoiding such research.

Data Sources

National Accounts in terms of local currency generally consist of data extracted from the World Bank's "Bank Economic and Social Data Base" (BESD) and from African Economic and Financial Data. Other national accounts are available from the United Nations'

System of National Accounts (SNA). National accounts data are converted into 1980 value US dollars. Conversion factors from World Bank and UNDP (1989a) were used to convert local currency GDP into constant value 1980 US dollars. The conversion factor is NOT identical to the official rate of exchange in a number of countries. In Angola, Cameroon, Equatorial Guinea, Gambia, Ghana, Guinea-Bissau, Somalia, Sudan and Uganda, official exchange rates were considered to be especially unrepresentative of rates effectively applied to international transactions as to be meaningless in cross country analysis. Instead, another exchange rate, one deemed to better represent the actual exchange rate at which most real international exchanges was used.

GDP Growth was calculated from annual observations of GDP using the least squares method discussed below. GDP data are from African Economic and Financial Data. GDP is represented by Q, and GDP average annual growth is represented by $\Delta Q/Q$.

Per Capita Incomes are in 1980 International dollars, calculated at purchasing power parity, from Summers and Heston (1988), except for Guinea-Bissau. Per capita income for Guinea-Bissau was taken from World Development Indicators ranking, and then interpolated to fit with the Summers and Heston data. Per capita income is represented by PCY.

Manufacturing Value-Added is also from World Bank data tapes, except for the Gambia. For the Gambia the ratio of manufacturing to GDP was taken for some years from the data annex of Sub-Saharan Africa:From Crisis to Sustained Growth, (1989) and then multiplied by the GDP values.

Investment defined as the change in gross fixed capital formation, data are from BESD include both private and public investment (governments and public enterprises and agencies). Data on private investment alone are not available. Investment is represented by ΔK.

Labor Force data from BESD represent total male and female of all age groups, of economically active populations. Data are reported for 1975, 1980 and 1985. Interpolations and extrapolations based on smooth growth rates were used to provide annual data. Labor force is represented by L.

Terms of Trade Adjuster was calculated from terms of trade and export ratios extracted from the diskette version of African Economic and Financial Data (AEFD), World Bank/UNDP (1989). The terms of trade adjuster is represented by ToT.

Black Market Exchange Rates are from the WORLD CURRENCY YEARBOOK various years, also known as Picks World Currency Yearbook.

Agricultural Export Values are from AEFD.

Government Expenditure data on the basis of the IMF's Government Financial Statistics Manual were downloaded through the World Bank's BESD, compared and corrected for with the GFS 1989 Yearbook, and brought as current as possible through reporting based on various country documents of the IMF such as, Recent Economic Developments (REDs), Article IV Consultations, etc. Data were also collected from World Bank documents and official country documents, such as budgets and outturn reports. These data, in general, are on cash and fiscal year bases, which for the majority of countries ends December 31. Government expenditures are represented by G.

Net Investment in Human Capital is the growth in Government education spending in real terms. Data are from the same source as government expenditure. Net Investment in Human Capital is represented by NIH.

Regime Indicators are from Gastil (1987), inverted and multiplied by 100, as discussed in chapter 3 and in Appendix 2. The regime indicator is represented by RD.

Homogeneity is meant to represent social or cultural homogeneity and is a crude attempt to include the concept of interest group behavior into the analysis. In fact, homogeneity is the inverse of the number of indigenous languages spoken in a country, where the more languages spoken the less homogeneity. Language numbers were taken from Morrison, Mitchell, and Paden (1989). Homogeneity is represented by HOM.

Methods

A variety of methods were used to aggregate data into the two time periods.

For investment, net investment in human capital, aggregate rents, changes in aggregate rents, government spending and the terms of trade adjuster annual observations were averaged for the two periods. If some observations were missing these were ignored. However, if only one or two observations were available the country case was dropped from the data set. Thus, some country cases are based on more available information than others. For instance, the change in aggregate rents as percent of GDP in Ghana for period 1 (1981-87) is based on observations for the entire period, whereas in Cote d' Ivoire, data are based on observations only through 1985, and for Lesotho, only through 1983. Obviously, the availability of data varies quite significantly from country to country, from variable to variable.

Average GDP and labor force growth are not averages of annual observations. Instead they are least squares growth rates: take the antilog of the coefficient of the following equation and subtract one to get the least squares growth rate $\ln Y = b_0 + b_1 \ln Time$, where Time is a vector $\{1,2,...n\}$.

Rent calculation has already been explained in Chapter 4.

The terms of trade adjuster,

$$TT = \frac{X}{Q} \times \frac{ToT_1}{ToT_0} - 1$$

and is similar to the methodology of the World Bank in adjusting GDP up to GDY, where X is exports and ToT is the international barter terms of trade. Indications are that the terms of trade adjusters were more negative in the 1981-87 period compared to 1975-81 period. In the earlier period trade terms were declining in 16 of 31 countries, while in the second period they were declining in 19 of 31 countries. Also, for all the countries together the average value in 1975-81 was -.0002, while in the later period it was -.0029, considerably worse.

RD (the regime indicator) was taken from Gastil's summary table of annual observations for two indicators of political freedom, each ranging from 1 to 7, with 7 being the worst. I averaged these observations for the two period (they do show some variation) then I inverted them. They were inverted so that the higher numbers would indicate greater and the lower numbers lesser political pluralism. These values were then multiplied by 100, simply to make them more manageable. There seems to be a slight worsening (diminishment) of political pluralism in the 1980s.

The SHOCK indicator was compiled from time-event lines from the World Bank's Social Development in Africa project. These time-event lines showed a variety of things: coups d' etat, war, drought, structural adjustment programs, low commodity prices, etc. I took only the negative, natural and man-made shocks. I did not include policy changes, new loans, etc. If a shock seemed to have a two year impact then it was assigned 2, a three year drought was assigned 3, a single coup attempts without great political instability afterwards was assigned a 1, and so on. There were more shocks in the second period than in the first.

Net Investment in Human Capital. There is ample justification for including human capital investment in any economic growth model. For instance T.W. Schultz (1961) pointed out a central role for "knowledge and similar attributes that affect human capabilities" as an important source of economic growth. It may be adequate to only look at investment in human capital in terms of education. While the case can be made for considering other types of "social welfare" or human capital spending, such as water and sanitary systems, many similar analyses are limited to education spending. In this paper only education spending is included, for three reasons: 1) other welfare spending in Africa varies in meaning from country to country; 2) information on education spending is often readily available, and even somewhat reliable; and 3) while health spending would be a reasonable input into human capital health spending by African governments (the only data available) probably provides at most 50 percent of all health spending, compared to education, where over 90 percent of primary school students attend government schools.

It is important that net investment in human capital be properly calculated, more so than for physical capital investment. The measure of human capital spending here is central government education spending. Generally, the percentage of GDP devoted to education has been used as a proxy for the growth inducing human capital investment variable. Barro (1989a&b) used government education spending as a percent of GDP and found no relationship to GDP growth. This is mistaken. Since most education spending merely serves to maintain the stock of human capital, or replace dying literates of earlier generations only the increase in education spending should be counted in net investment in human capital.

To correct for this let H_0 represent the entire amount spent to educate the initial cohort and H_1 the amount spent to educate the next cohort. Assume there are two cohorts, one of school age and the other of working age. Of the working population only the literates embody human capital and they are homogenous as a productive factor. The illiterates are homogeneously without human capital, embodying solely brute labor. There is no population growth.

Gross investment in human capital is the cost of educating to literacy the school aged children who attend school. Only when more children are educated beyond the numbers of literate adults who die is there a net increase in the stock of human capital. Those literate children who, upon entering the working age population, only offset the deaths of the adult illiterates do not increase the stock of human capital.

If we assume that education (as investment in human capital) has constant returns then only that part of education spending that adds to the stock of human capital should be seen as investment. Thus, net investment in human capital is the change in education spending rather than the absolute amount of education spending, i.e., $NIH = H_1 - H_0$. Therefore, instead of using the ratio of government education spending in GDP as the investment in human capital variable (as does Barro 1989a&b), I use the change in government education spending as a share of GDP averaged yearly.

Tables

The following tables present the data used in this book, as well as the matrix of correlations among the variables. Complete (or near complete) data sets are available only for 21 countries over the two periods, making for a maximum of 42 observations on the complete general model. Annual data for each indicator are available in Gallagher (Spring 1991).

Table A.1: Matrix of Correlations among Variables:
(in percentage terms)

	ΔL/Q	ΔR1/Q	ΔR2/Q	G/Q	ΔQ/Q	HOM
ΔG/Q	-26	29	28	25	63	-40
ΔL/Q		-49	-51	-57	-57	-32
ΔR1/Q			100	98	49	-50
ΔR2/Q				98	50	-48
G/Q					49	-51
ΔQ/Q						-40

	ΔK/Q	ΔL/L	NIH/Q	PCY	R1/Q	R2/Q
ΔG/Q	49	-03	62	34	10	14
ΔL/Q	-64	-25	-27	-85	-41	-43
ΔR1/Q	79	67	85	84	91	92
ΔR2/Q	76	68	82	86	93	94
G/Q	75	63	78	85	92	93
ΔQ/Q	82	08	55	59	43	45
HOM	-42	-28	-66	-11	-49	-48

	RD	SK	TIME	dU/Q	TT	
ΔG/Q	36	39	33	60	-43	
ΔL/Q	-35	56	-34	-62	44	
ΔR1/Q	84	-22	20	71	-25	
ΔR2/Q	84	-24	22	72	-20	
G/Q	80	-31	17	70	-21	
ΔQ/Q	61	-39	-20	96	-17	
HOM	-65	-17	31	-48	-06	

continuation of Table A.1: Matrix of Correlations among Variables:

	ΔL/L	NIH/Q	PCY	R1/Q	R2/Q	RD
ΔK/Q	31	80	74	60	61	76
ΔL/L		37	61	81	78	78
NIH/Q			58	62	64	74
PCY				80	82	70
R1/Q					100	87
R2/Q						85
	SK	TIME	dU/Q	TT		
dK/Q	-36	-12	90	-46		
dL/L	-19	37	28	-18		
NIH/Q	18	13	70	-36		
PCY	-46	40	75	-36		
R1/Q	-38	16	64	02		
R2/Q	-35	19	66	03		
RD	-25	03	76	-25		
SK		38	-39	-08		
TIME			-08	-32		
TT				-20		

Table A.2: Master Data Set: 1975-81 (R is R1 only)

Country	ΔQ/Q	ΔR/Q	ΔU/Q	ΔK/Q	ΔL/L	NIH/Q
Benin	4.8			21.0	2.2	-0.07
Botswana	11.9	4.2	15.9	40.3	3.0	1.2
Burkina Faso	3.3			24.9	1.9	0.14
Burundi	4.5	0.4	4.8	12.6	1.4	0.44
Cameroon	12.1	-0.2	12.1	21.3	1.6	-0.03
CAR	0.0			10.7	1.3	
Chad	-5.4	-0.2	-5.5	18.6	1.8	-0.04
Congo	6.6			33.4	2.1	
Cote d' Ivoire	4.4			26.3	2.4	2.2
Ethiopia	2.9			9.3	2.0	0.03
Gabon	-4.8			45.6	0.9	
Gambia	3.0			20.9	1.8	0.6
Ghana	1.4	-0.6	0.9	8.0	2.7	-0.43
Guinea	3.3	0.6	3.9	14.4	1.8	
Guinea-Bissau	0.0			21.7	4.1	
Kenya	5.9			24.7	3.7	0.3
Lesotho	9.2	3.0	12.2	30.0	2.1	0.03
Liberia	1.9			28.7	2.6	0.5
Madagascar	0.5	-0.8	-0.5	17.3	2.2	-0.5
Malawi	4.0			28.0	2.6	0.3
Mali	4.5	0.6	5.1	16.3	2.0	0.0

cont.A.2, 75-81	ΔQ/Q	ΔR/Q	ΔU/Q	ΔK/Q	ΔL/L	NIH/Q
Mauritania	2.6	-1.3	1.5	35.6	1.9	-0.1
Mauritius	3.6			28.0	3.4	0.5
Niger	6.8	-1.4	6.1	22.0	2.1	0.12
Nigeria	2.3	-0.6	2.2	23.3	3.2	-0.13
Rwanda	8.5	-0.6	8.5	14.4	3.2	0.44
Senegal	0.4			16.1	3.1	0.3
Sierra Leone	2.0			14.1	1.0	0.2
Somalia	4.9	-1.0	3.9	19.9	3.4	0.1
Sudan	2.1	0.3	2.4	16.3	2.7	0.2
Swaziland	2.4	1.0	3.4	33.0	2.2	0.7
Tanzania	1.7			23.6	2.9	0.0
Togo	4.3	-0.2	4.0	34.6	2.2	0.6
Uganda	-4.4	-0.9	-5.7	6.7	2.9	-0.3
Zaire	-0.8	0.7	-0.6	14.6	1.9	0.2
Zambia	0.4	-1.1	-0.7	24.3	2.9	-0.2
Zimbabwe	1.9	-0.7	1.3	18.6	2.9	0.6
	ΔG/Q	R/Q	G/Q	ΔL/Q	PCY	SHOCK
Benin	-2.1		23.5	34.8	589	0
Botswana	0.6	28.0	41.8	12.5	1107	1
Burkina Faso	0.8		16.5	51.2	329	1
Burundi	0.4	11.6	22.3	34.7	294	3
Cameroon	0.3	13.1	16.6	9.6	756	0
CAR			21.4	18.9	491	0
Chad	-0.8	11.2	15.7	32.5	461	4
Congo	-5.0		40.3	9.0	859	0
Cote d' Ivoire	2.5	17.6	34.7	8.2	1050	0
Ethiopia	1.8		22.2	85.7	329	4

cont.A.2, 75-81	ΔG/Q	R/Q	G/Q	ΔL/Q	PCY	SHOCK
Gabon	1.6		41.7	0.9	3099	0
Gambia	2.4		27.9	21.6	560	0
Ghana	-0.8	15.5	17.3	25.25	495	0
Guinea		20.2		27.4	409	0
Guinea-Bissau	-18.3		63.7	117.8	329	3
Kenya	1.4		26.0	37.2	603	0
Lesotho	4.6	18.5	46.8	40.7	540	0
Liberia	2.1		26.6	16.1	681	2
Madagascar	3.0	12.4		27.4	593	0
Malawi	1.9		30.3	56.9	409	2
Mali		8.2	17.0	28.4	323	0
Mauritania	-0.4	22.0	44.0	14.0	600	3
Mauritius	2.2		29.3	09.2	1367	0
Niger	1.4	6.1	17.1	25.6	361	0
Nigeria	1.6	14.4	22.4	9.6	705	0
Rwanda	0.8	9.6	14.2	79.5	350	1
Senegal	0.9		21.2	25.1	758	2
Sierra Leone	0.6		27.3	12.2	495	1
Somalia	-0.7	8.1	18.3	35.6	409	2
Sudan	0.5	12.7	20.7	22.6	645	0
Swaziland	1.7	17.6	33.3	9.5	1041	0
Tanzania	0.3		28.9	52.0	318	3
Togo	-1.7	11.4	42.8	23.3	663	0
Uganda	-1.5	13.6	9.6	81.6	347	3
Zaire	-0.9	19.4	18.3	18.4	354	2
Zambia	0.8	27.3	40.4	12.9	883	0
Zimbabwe	0.2	20.3	32.0	15.6	1000	2

cont.A.2, 75-81	RD	HOM	TT			
Benin	7	6.67	0.71			
Botswana	20	50.00	-1.46			
Burkina Faso	12	3.70	-0.04			
Burundi	8	50.00	1.32			
Cameroon	9	2.00	1.38			
CAR	7	2.44	1.12			
Chad	8	4.55				
Congo	8	14.29	5.37			
Cote d' Ivoire	9	1.75	1.09			
Ethiopia	8	1.59	0.91			
Gabon	8	6.67				
Gambia	25	16.67	-0.48			
Ghana	10	2.70	0.35			
Guinea	7	4.55				
Guinea-Bissau	8	16.67				
Kenya	10	4.55	0.04			
Lesotho	11	50.00	-0.07			
Liberia	10	3.45	-2.58			
Madagascar	9	100.0	0.19			
Malawi	8	20.00	-0.77			
Mali	7	6.67	-0.07			
Mauritania	8	50.00	-1.98			
Mauritius	20		-3.32			
Niger	8	7.14	-1.04			
Nigeria	12	0.80	2.69			
Rwanda	8	50.00	0.38			
Senegal	11	12.50	-0.68			

cont.A.2, 75-81	RD	HOM	TT			
Sierra Leone	10	12.50	-0.02			
Somalia	7	50.00	0.24			
Sudan	9	0.58	0.12			
Swaziland	10	33.33				
Tanzania	8	1.79	0.03			
Togo	8	1.79	-1.57			
Uganda	8	4.17				
Zaire	8	1.64	-0.38			
Zambia	10	1.45	-1.28			
Zimbabwe	10	33.33	-0.87			

150

Continuation of A.2, data for 1981-87 (R is R1 only)						
Country	ΔQ/Q	ΔR/Q	ΔU/Q	ΔK/Q	ΔL/L	NIH/Q
Benin	2.9			16.1	2.0	
Botswana	12.4	4.1	16.5	27.3	3.5	0.8
Burkina Faso	6.3			20.6	1.9	0.1
Burundi	4.0	-0.1	3.9	16.7	2.0	
Cameroon	7.5	0.3	7.8	21.6	1.8	0.29
CAR	1.8			11.9	1.3	
Chad	3.7	-0.1	3.5	8.4	1.8	0.25
Congo	7.0			37.0	1.8	
Cote d' Ivoire	1.2	2.7	4.1	16.9	2.7	0.32
Ethiopia	0.6			11.4	1.7	0.24
Gabon	2.4			36.1	0.6	
Gambia	2.4			21.3	1.2	0.03
Ghana	1.0	-0.3	0.8	7.1	2.7	0.22
Guinea	6.3	2.4	8.7	13.4	1.6	
Guinea-Bissau	1.7			27.1	1.1	-0.43
Kenya	3.2			23.1	3.5	0.32
Lesotho	1.7	6.7	7.5	32.6	2.0	0.23
Liberia	1.4			10.1	2.2	0.3
Madagascar	1.1	-0.2	0.9	14.3	1.9	-0.25
Malawi	3.2			16.6	2.6	0.07
Mali	2.5	0.8	3.3	18.6	2.5	0.0

cont.A.2, 81-87	ΔQ/Q	ΔR/Q	ΔU/Q	ΔK/Q	ΔL/L	NIH/Q
Mauritania	1.3	3.2	4.4	28.4	2.7	
Mauritius	4.2			21.9	3.3	-0.07
Niger	-1.8	-0.2	-1.9	12.3	2.3	-0.17
Nigeria	-1.3	-0.7	-1.6	13.0	2.6	-0.80
Rwanda	2.9	0.4	3.3	15.9	2.8	0.23
Senegal	2.9			14.9	1.9	-0.17
Sierra Leone	-0.8			11.7	1.1	-0.24
Somalia	1.2	0.2	1.4	10.9	2.0	-0.05
Sudan	0.9	-0.5	0.4	15.1	2.8	
Swaziland	2.4	0.6	3.0	16.1	2.2	0.23
Tanzania	1.6			17.3	2.8	-0.43
Togo	-0.1	0.2	0.2	22.6	2.2	0.12
Uganda	-1.0			9.7	2.7	-0.02
Zaire	1.5	-0.9	0.3	13.0	2.3	-0.01
Zambia	-0.4	1.0	0.0	15.7	3.2	-0.14
Zimbabwe	2.8	3.8	6.7	19.9	2.7	0.59
	ΔG/Q	R/Q	G/Q	ΔL/Q	PCY	SHOCK
Benin	-2.6		24.5	28.5	555	0
Botswana	1.0	36.9	45.6	9.5	1450	1
Burkina Faso	0.4		17.3	45.4	369	5
Burundi	1.0	9.1	26.1	45.4	358	3
Cameroon	1.1	7.8	21.2	6.9	931	2
CAR	-1.2		16.0	19.8	466	3
Chad	8.4	9.9	21.1	37.1	312	3
Congo	-2.2		40.6	4.8	981	0
Cote d' Ivoire	-0.5	24.2	35.5	9.3	1101	1
Ethiopia	1.4		32.2	70.2	318	3

cont.A.2, 81-87	ΔG/Q	R/Q	G/Q	ΔL/Q	PCY	SHOCK
Gabon	0.4		41.2	0.7	3247	0
Gambia	-0.3		30.3	13.8	602	1
Ghana	0.5	11.2	11.9	29.1	389	4
Guinea		27.6	20.7	23.9	448	1
Guinea-Bissau	-2.3		54.1	35.2	311	1
Kenya	0.4		27.5	34.1	652	2
Lesotho	-0.4	27.5	52.2	35.3	692	2
Liberia	-0.5		30.3	16.0	578	2
Madagascar	0.7	10.7	21.4	27.7	542	0
Malawi	-1.1		31.2	58.2	392	2
Mali		9.7	29.6	33.5	343	5
Mauritania	-1.7	28.9	39.3	20.1	571	2
Mauritius	-1.1		28.0	8.8	1688	0
Niger	0.2	5.6	20.3	29.2	456	3
Nigeria	0.8	10.6	20.2	10.1	726	0
Rwanda	1.2	9.0	20.0	60.0	377	4
Senegal	-0.4		24.0	15.2	730	2
Sierra Leone	-0.2		22.0	13.0	502	1
Somalia	1.9	5.7	21.2	23.1	409	2
Sudan	-0.3	11.8	20.3	26.5	674	5
Swaziland	-0.3	22.6	34.3	9.3	1138	1
Tanzania	-1.0		24.6	54.3	329	1
Togo	-0.2	10.2	34.1	25.3	576	3
Uganda	0.1		10.3	90.0	271	3
Zaire	1.4	16.7	22.7	23.3	233	0
Zambia	-1.1	18.6	36.2	17.1	711	4
Zimbabwe	1.9	22.7	40.0	13.9	1010	5

cont.A.2, 81-87	RD	HOM	TT			
Benin	7	6.67	-0.36			
Botswana	20	50.00	0.35			
Burkina Faso	8	3.70	0.06			
Burundi	8	50.00	0.03			
Cameroon	8	2.00	-2.40			
CAR	8	2.44	-0.16			
Chad	8	4.55				
Congo	8	14.29	-3.46			
Cote d' Ivoire	9	1.75	0.38			
Ethiopia	7	1.59	0.18			
Gabon	8	6.67				
Gambia	17	16.67	-0.12			
Ghana	10	2.70	0.16			
Guinea	8	4.55				
Guinea-Bissau	8	16.67				
Kenya	10	4.55	0.14			
Lesotho	10	50.00	-0.37			
Liberia	9	3.45	0.89			
Madagascar	9	100.0	-0.02			
Malawi	8	20.00	-0.46			
Mali	8	6.67	-0.14			
Mauritania	8	50.00	-0.61			
Mauritius	22		1.13			
Niger	8	7.14	-0.56			
Nigeria	12	0.80	-1.17			
Rwanda	8	50.00	0.26			
Senegal	13	12.50	-0.56			

cont.A.2, 81-87	RD	HOM	TT			
Sierra Leone	10	12.50	-0.13			
Somalia	7	50.00	-0.03			
Sudan	9	0.58	-0.12			
Swaziland	10	33.33				
Tanzania	8	1.79	0.13			
Togo	8	1.79	-1.63			
Uganda	11	4.17				
Zaire	8	1.64	-0.51			
Zambia	8	1.45	0.09			
Zimbabwe	11	33.33	-0.02			

Appendix 2

Notes on African Regimes

This appendix provides the reader with more information on African regimes in a very summary form. The appendix can serve the reader as a quick reference on African regimes and their characteristics as well as provide a link between these characteristics and the numerical rankings used in this book.

Information on African regimes is available from a number of sources. In the end the data from Gastil (1987) were selected for use in the quantitative analysis. The reasons for this choice are given in the last paragraph of this section. There is a variety of ways to classify, categorize or fit index numbers to African regimes. Three source that have done this are discussed briefly and are summarized below. These are Chazan et al. (1988), the World Human Rights Guide (1987), and the Political Handbook of the World (1988).

Chazan et al. (1988) categorized African regimes as below. The categories are fully discussed in Chapter 3. Table A2.1 presents African regimes as classified by Chazan et al. and are ranked by likely degree of institutional competition for rents, as discussed in Chapter 3.

The Chazan regime categories are briefly recapped here:

(1) Pluralistic: competition among political parties, and separation of powers among the legislative, executive, and judicial branches of government;

(2) Administrative-hegemonical: there is still some political competition, although there may only be one party. Most decision-making in hands of the executive, although bureaucracy may make technical decisions, with national defense left to the military. Judiciary retains some degree of autonomy;

(3) Populist: usually transitional, having taken power from rather dictatorial and unpopular regimes. Often reformist but retaining centralized power structures;

(4) Party-centrist: centralize power around the party and the party's ideals. No room for competition from outside of the party and little room even within the party. Much power is retain by the executive;

(5) Party-mobilizing: power is also centralized around the party and its ideals. But, there may be greater competition within the party compared to the party-centrist regime, and there is less dominance by the executive;

(6) Personal-coercive: strong leaders, in terms of power and ruthlessness, maintain strict control over the military and the police, rule by the edict (often, executive order) and allow no opposition from within or outside the party; and

(7) Ambiguous: exhibit too much instability and anarchy to discern much of a real political process.

Table A2.1: Institutional Competition and Regime Type:

Degree of Competition	Regime type	Degree of Competition	Regime type
High		Low	
Botswana	Pluralist	Angola	Party-centrist
the Gambia	"	Benin	"
Mauritius	"	Congo	"
Senegal	"	Guinea-Bissau	"
Intermediate	"	Ethiopia	"
Ghana (Rawlings)	Populist	Mozambique	"
Cote d' Ivoire	Administrative-hegemonical	Ghana (Nkrumah)	Party-mobilizing
Cameroon	"	Guinea	"
Liberia (pre-1980)	"	Tanzania	"
Malawi	"	Zimbabwe	"
Kenya	"	Mali	"
Nigeria	"	Uganda (Amin)*	Personal-coercive
Senegal	"	Uganda* (1980s)	ambiguous
Togo	"	CAR (Bokassa)	Personal-coercive
Zaire	"	Equatorial Guinea	"
Zambia	"	Liberia (Doe)	"
		Burkina Faso	Populist
		Chad*	ambiguous
		Sudan*	"

* These countries experienced such instability in their social,
political and economic systems that they are classified as anarchic.
Source: Regime Types from Chazan, Mortimer, Ravenhill and Rothchild (1988).

This categorization of African countries, while useful, does not directly indicate the degree of competition among institutions, although it is a valuable source of practical information. The World Human Rights Guide (1986) provides considerably more relevant and systematic information, although for fewer countries.

The World Human Rights Guide (WHRG) surveyed human rights in 120 countries, although its full survey was only conducted for 90 of these. For the other 30 a brief survey was conducted. The full survey assigned weighted averages of values-attached questions. For instance, the survey asks about "Freedom from or rights to peaceful political opposition." An affirmative answer rates 2, an affirmative answer with qualification rates 1, and a negative answer rates 0. The survey consists of forty questions, of which nine are directly relevant to the degree of competition among state institutions. The results of the comprehensive survey are found in table A.1, while the results and comments from a less comprehensive survey follow the table.

The results of this survey as related to the nine areas listed below. Scores of 1, 2, or 3 are assigned. The survey does not cover all countries of Africa. However, the shortened survey in WHRG does provide comments on several other countries, some of which are ranked as POOR (indicating poor status of civil and political rights) or BAD (which is worse). Comments on other countries are from the Political Handbook of the World 1988. scores for some of those will be based on other data, such as data from the shortened survey or scores derived from above.

Table A2.2: Political and Civil Rights in Africa
             (Scores 0=poor, 1=medium, 2=good)
    Survey areas of investigation:
A. Free to teach ideas and receive information.
B. Extra-legal killings or "disappearances" by government.
C. Compulsory membership in state organizations or parties.
D. Press censorship.
E. Peaceful political opposition.
F. Multiparty elections by secret and universal ballot
G. Independent newspapers.
H. Independent radio and TV.
I. Courts have autonomy from political control or from other aspects
of the state.

country	score	A	B	C	D	E	F	G	H	I
Senegal	1.7	2	2	2	2	2	2	1	2	1
Botswana	1.7	1	2	2	2	2	2	2	1	1
Sierra L.	0.9	1	1	1	2	1	0	0	1	1
Liberia	0.9	1	0	1	2	1	1	0	1	1
Zimbabwe	0.8	0	1	0	2	1	1	1	1	0
Nigeria	0.8	1	1	2	0	1	0	0	1	1
Zambia	0.7	0	1	2	1	1	0	0	1	0
Kenya	0.7	1	1	1	1	1	1	0	1	0
Cameroon	0.7	1	1	1	1	1	0	0	1	0
Benin	0.7	1	1	2	2	0	0	0	0	0
Ghana	0.7	1	1	0	2	1	0	0	1	0
Tanzania	0.5	0	1	2	1	0	0	0	0	0
Zaire	0.3	1	0	1	0	0	0	0	1	0
Ethiopia	0.1	0	0	0	1	0	0	0	0	0

Table A2.3: Summary of Comments on Political and Civil Rights in Africa from the World Human Rights Guide

Burkina Faso	Poor	Military government, there is little political opposition, many attempted coups.
Burundi	Poor	One party state, no legal political opposition, no freedom of the press.
Cote d' Ivoire	Poor	One party state, very powerful president, some press freedom.
Guinea	Poor	Until 1984 the country had been run at the discretion of Sekou Toure with only one party and tight "African Socialist" control of the economy. Since 1984 there has been some liberalization of the economy and political power is in the hands of the military.
Lesotho	Poor	One party state, limited press freedoms, independent courts.
Madagascar	Poor	One party state but coalition politics, limited press freedoms.
Malawi	Poor	President for life, one party, no legal opposition, no free press.
Mali	Poor	One party state with military wing, no opposition and no press freedom.
Niger	Poor	Military government, president rules by decree, no opposition, courts are controlled by the president.
Rwanda	Poor	One party state, no opposition, government controls the courts.
Somalia	Poor	Single party, powerful president, no legal opposition. At the end of 1990 the country slipped into anarchy.
Sudan	Poor	President for 24 years was overthrown in military coup in 1985. Courts are not free. Imposition of Sharia (Islamic law) incites protest from non-Islamic south. Country has been experiencing civil war and anarchy on and off for past thirty years.

continuation of table A2.3		
Country	Score	Comments
Togo	Poor	Absolute one party rule. No legal opposition, no press freedoms, and no free courts.
Uganda	Poor	Post-colonial history marked by genocide, dictatorial rule and anarchy. Many signs that the 1980s have seen considerable improvements in basic human rights.
Central African Rep.	Bad	History of dictatorship and single party rule. For a time Known as Central African Empire under Emperor Bokasa, one of Africa's most notorious dictators. No free press, opposition, nor courts. Close to anarchic.

Source: Comments are summarized from Humana, The World Human Rights Guide (1986).

The next set of comments is drawn from the Political Handbook of the World. These comments include those countries that were not covered in the World Human Rights Guide survey. The Political Handbook of the World does not include scores or grades for countries and their political and civil rights.

162

Table A2.4: Summary of Comments from the Political Handbook of the World

Country	Comments
Mauritius	Multi-party parliamentary system, free press, and as a participating member of the Commonwealth the judicial system allows for appeal to the United Kingdom Privy Council.
Chad	History of military regimes. No free press, legislature was dissolved in 1975, no legal opposition. The country has been close to anarchy for much of its post-colonial history.
Congo	One party state, no free press, no free opposition, revolutionary courts of justice, media subject to government censors.
Gabon	On party state, no legal opposition, all news media owned and controlled by the government.
the Gambia	The country regularly holds popular elections, there is free press and legal political opposition.
Guinea-Bissau	Revolutionary council runs the affairs of government. There is limited press freedom and no legal political opposition.
Mauritania	One party state under military rule, no legal opposition, no legislature since 1978, no free press.
Seychelles	One party state but with popular elections since 1979. No legal opposition. Coercive press censorship.
Swaziland	Constitutional monarchy. One party state although there are opposition parties. Press is privately owned and free.

Source: comments are summarized from Banks, Political Handbook of the World (1988)

Data from Gastil (1987) 1986 survey and ratings of countries since 1973 yield composite indicators on an annual basis from 1973,

1975-1986. These data were manipulated slightly to provide the indicator of the degree of institutional competition for rents found in Table 3.2 and used for Figure 3.2 and used in the regressions of chapter 4. The data were averaged 1975-81, 1981-86 for a single period value, inverted (so that the most pluralistic countries would have the highest numbers) and multiplied by 100. Although essentially very similar to the above indicators, the survey covers all but 1987 of the period for this research. The Gastil index also covers all the countries of Sub-Saharan Africa, whereas the World Human Rights Guide and the Political Handbook of the World cover fewer countries and do not provide results for annual coverage. For these reasons, the Gastil index was selected for this analysis.

Bibliography

Abramovitz, M. (1952) "Economics of Growth," in B. Haley ed. A Survey of Contemporary Economics: Vol. II, published for the American Economics Association by Richard D. Irwin, Inc.

Abramovitz, M. (1962) "Review of Denison," American Economic Review, September.

Adelman, I. (1961) Theories of Economic Growth and Development Stanford University Press: Stanford, CA.

Agarwala, R. (1983) Price Distortions and Growth in Developing Countries, World Bank Staff Working Paper no. 575.

Alchian, A. and H. Demsetz (1972) "Production, Information Costs, and Economic Organization," American Economic Review, 62:777-795.

Anam, M. (1982) "Distortion-Triggered Lobbying and Welfare: A Contribution to the Theory of Directly-Unproductive Profit-Seeking Activities," Journal of International Economics, 13: 15-32.

___ and E. Katz (1988) "Rent-seeking and Second Best Economics," Public Choice, 59: 215-224.

Anderson, D. (1987) Economic Growth and the Returns to Investment, World Bank Discussion Paper No. 12.

Appelbaum, E. and E. Katz (1987 or so) "Seeking Rents by Setting Rents: The Political Economy of Rent-Seeking," Economic Journal, 97: 685-699

Arrau, P. (1989) "Human Capital and Endogenous Growth in a Large-Scale Life-Cycle Model," World Bank, Working Papers Series No. 342.

Ashoff, G. (1988) "Rent-Seeking: Zur Relevanz eines relativ neuen Konzeptes in der oekonomischen Theorie der Politik und der entwicklungstheoretischen Diskussion," Vierteljahresberichte, Probleme der internationalen Zusammenarbeit, (FRG) No. 112: 103-25, June.

Baldwin, R. (1984) "Rent-Seeking and Trade Policy: an Industry Approach," National Bureau of Economic Research, Working Paper Series No. 1499: 1-26, November.

Banks, A. ed. (1988) Political Handbook of the World 1988, CSA Publications, State University of New York at Binghamton.

Bardhan, P. (1988) "Alternative Approaches to Development," in J. Bhagwati and T.N. Srinivasan eds Handbook of Development Economics.

Barro, R. (1989a) A Cross-Country Study of Growth, Saving and Government, February, National Bureau of Economic Research, Working Paper No. 2855.

___ (1989b) "Economic Growth in a Cross Section of Countries," Prepared for a conference on human capital and growth, SUNY Buffalo, May.

Bates, R. (1972) Markets and the State in Tropical Africa, University of California Press.

Becker, G. (1964) Human Capital: A Theoretical and Empirical Analysis, with Special Reference to Education, New York and London: Columbia University Press for the National Bureau of Economic Research.

___ (1967) "Optimal Investment in Human Capital," reproduced in (1971) B. F. Kiker ed. Investment in Human Capital, University of South Carolina Press.

___ (1989) Kevin M. Murphy, and Robert Tamura, Human Capital Fertility and Economic Growth, Population Research Center Discussion Paper Series, Economic Demography Group, Economics Research Center, NORC/University of Chicago: Chicago, IL.

Beenstock, M. (1989) "A Democratic Model of the 'Rent-Sought' Benefit Cycle," Public Choice, 63: 1-14.

Belsley, David (1982) "Assessing the Presence of Harmful Collinearity and Other Forms of Weak Data through a Test for Signal-to-Noise," Journal of Econometrics, (Nov.) pp. 211-253.

Benson, B. and J. Mitchell (1988) "Rent-Seekers Who Demand Government Production: Bureaucratic Output and the Price of Complements," Public Choice, 56: 3-16.

Berry, J. (1970) "Language Systems and Literature," a chapter in J. Paden and E. Soja eds. The African Experience, Volume I: Essays.

Bhagwati, J. and T.N. Srinivasan (1980) "Revenue Seeking: A Generalization of the Theory of Tariffs," Journal of Political Economy, 90: 988-1002.

___ (1982) "Directly Unproductive Profit-Seeking (DUP) Activities," Journal of Political Economy, vol. 90, no. 5: 988-1002.

___ and P. Desai (1970) Planning for Industrialization: A Study of India's Trade and Industrial Policies Since 1950, Oxford Univewrsity Press, Oxford, for the Development Centre of the OECD.

Blomqvist, A. and S. Mohammad (1986) "Controls, Corruption, and Competitive Rent-Seeking in LDCs," Journal of Development Economics, 21: 161-180.

Branson, W. (1979) Macroeconomic Theory and Policy 2nd ed. Harper and Row Publishers.

Britto, R., (1973) "Some Recent Developments in the Theory of Economic Growth," Journal of Economic Literature, December: 1343-1366.

Bruno, M. (1968) "Estimation of Factor Contribution to Growth under Structural Disequilibrium," International Economic Review, 1: Feb: 49-62.

Buchanan, J. (1980) "Rent Seeking and Profit Seeking," in Toward a Theory of the Rent-Seeking Society, ed. J. Buchanan, R. Tollison, and G. Tullock, pp. 3-15, College Station: Texas A&M University Press.

___ (1984) "Politics without Romance: A Sketch of Positive Public Choice Theory and Its Normative Implications," reprinted in J. Buchanan and R. Tollison eds. The Theory of Public Choice-II, The University of Michigan Press.

___ and R. Wagner (1977) Democracy in Deficit, New York: Academic Press.

___ and G. Tullock, (1962) The Calculus of Consent, Ann Arbor: University of Michigan Press.

___, R. Tollison, and G. Tullock, eds. (1980) Toward a Theory of the Rent-Seeking Society, College Station, Texas A&M University Press.

Chander, R. (1990) "Information Systems and Basic Statistics in Sub-Saharan Africa: A Review and Strategy for Improvement," World Bank Discussion Paper No. 73.

Chazan, N., R. Mortimer, J. Ravenhill and D. Rothchild, (1988) Politics and Society in Contemporary Africa, Lynne Rienner Publishers.

Choi, K. (1983) "A Statistical Test of Olson's Model, in Dennis Mueller ed. The Political Economy of Growth.

Christ, Carl F. (1966) Econometric Models and Methods, New York: Wiley and Sons, Inc.

Clarete, R. and J. Whalley (1985) Interactions between the Trade Policies and Domestic Distortion, Centre for the Study of International Economic Relations, Working Paper 8522C, London, Ontario: University of Western Ontario.

Cleaves, S. (1980) "Implementation Amidst Scarcity and Apathy: Political Power and Policy Design," in M.S. Grindle ed. Politics and Policy Implementation in the Third World, Princeton University Press.

Congelton, R. (1980) "Competitive Process, Competitive Waste, and Institutions," in Buchanan, Tullock , and Tollison op. cit.

Corden, W. M. (1987) "The Relevance for Developing Countries of Recent Developments in Macroeconomic Theory," The World Bank Research Observer, Vol. 2, No. 2, July.

Cowitt, P. ed. (1989) 1986-87 World Currency Yearbook, International Currency Analysis, Inc. Brooklyn, NY., and earlier editions also referred to as The Picks Currency Yearbook.

Crain, W.M. and A. Zardkoohi (1980) "X-Efficiency and Nonpecuniary Rewards in a Rent-Seeking Society: A Neglected Issue in theProperty Rights Theory of the Firm," American Economic Review, 70: 784-792.

___ and R. Tollison (1979) "Constitutional Change in an Interest-Group Perspective," Journal of Legal Studies, 8:165-75.

Denison, Edward F. (1974) Acccounting for United States Growth 1929-1969, Washington D.C.: The Brookings Institution.

Dervis, K., J. De Melo and S. Robinson (1982) General Models for Development Policy, Cambridge University Press, New York, for the World Bank.

Domar, E. (1947) "Expansion and Employment," American Economic Review, March.

Doran, Howard E. (1979) Applied Regression Analysis in Econometrics New York: Marcel Dekker, Inc.

Easterly, W., (1989) "Policy Distortions, Size of Government, and Growth," November 10, mimeo, World Bank.

___ and D. Wetzel, (1989), "Policy Determinants of Growth: Survey of Theory and Evidence," background paper for Chapter 8 of the Second Review of Adjustment Lending, Oct. 3, World Bank, and published as a World Bank Working Paper Series No. 343.

Edwards, S., (1988a) "Notes on Openness, Outward Orientation, Trade Liberalization and Economic Performance in Developing Countries," (an "incomplete first draft") June, National Bureau of Economic Research.

___ (1988b) "Stabilization, Macroeconomic Policy and Trade Liberalization," (Preliminary first draft) National Bureau of Economic Research, May.

Ekelund, R. and R. Tollison (1981) Mercantilism as a Rent-Seeking Society: Economic Regulation in Historical Perspective, Texas A & M.

Feder, G. (1983) "On Exports and Economic Growth," Journal of Development Economics, 12: 59-73.

Findlay, R. (1989) Is the New Political Economy Relevant to Developing Countries? Working Paper Series (WPS 292), The World Bank.

Fisher, F. (1985) "The Social Costs of Monopoly and Regulation: Posner Reconsidered,"Journal of Political Economy, 92: 410-416.

Fomby, Thomas B., R. Carter Hill, and Stanley R. Johnson (1984) Advanced Econometric Methods, New York: Springer-Verlag Inc.

Formby, J., J. Keeler and P. Thistle (1988) "X-efficiency, Rent-Seeking and Social Costs," Public Choice, 57: 115-126.

Frey, B. and F. Schneider (1975) "On the Modelling of Politico-Economic Interdependence," Economic Journal of Political Research, 3: 339-360.

Friedman, M. (1957) A Theory of the Consumption Function, Princeton University Press.

Gallagher, M. (1989) "Fiscal Contraction and the Social Sectors in Developing Countries," a background paper for the 1990 World Development Report, World Bank.

___ and O. Ogbu (1989) "Public Expenditures, Resource Use and the Social Sectors in Sub-Saharan Africa," mimeo.

___ (1990/91) "Scorecard of Economic Reforms," Fletcher Forum of World Affairs, Special Africa Issue, Winter.

___ (1991) Rent-Seeking and Economic Growth in Africa, Ph.D. dissertation, George Mason University, Fairfax, VA. Spring

Gastil, R. (1987) Freedom in the World, Greenwood Press, Westport CT.

Gelb, A., J. Knight, and R. Sabot (1988) "Lewis Through a Loooking Glass: Public Sector Employment, Rent-Seeking and Economic Growth," World Bank Working Paper Series No. 133, November.

Gemmel, N. (1983) "International Comparisons of the Effects of Nonmarket-Sector Growth," Journal of Comparative Economics no. 7: 368-381.

Glade, W. (1989) "Privatization in Rent-Seeking Societies," World Development, 17: 673-82, May.

Grais, W., J. Demelo, and U. Shujiro (1986) "A General Equilibrium Estimation of the Effects of Reduction in Tariffs and Quantitative Restrictions in Turkey in 1978," in T.N. Srinivasan and J. Whalley eds. General Equilibrium Trade Policy Modelling, Cambridge, MA: MIT Press.

Grier, K. and G. Tullock (1989) "An Empirical Analysis of Cross-National Economic Growth, 1951-80," Journal of Monetary Economics, 24: 259-276

Grindle, M. (1990) "The New Political Economy: Positive Economics and Negative Politics," World Bank Staff Working Papers, WPS 304.

Grossman, P. (1988) "Government and economic growth: A non-linearrelationship," Public Choice 56: 193-200.

Hahn, F. and R. Matthews, (1965) "The Theory of Economic Growth: A Survey," in N. Buchanan ed. Surveys of Economic Growth: Growth and Development: Vol. II, prepared for the American Economic Association and the Royal Economic Society, St. Martin's Press: New York.

Harberger, A. (1954) "Monopoly and Resource Allocation," American Economic Review, 74: 660-672.

___ (1959) "Using the Resources at Hand More Effectively," American Economic Review vol. 49, no. 2, May.

Harrod, R. (1959) "Domar and Dynamic Economics," Economic Journal,September.

Healey, D. (1977) "Development Policy: New Thinking about an Interpretation," Journal of Economic Literature, 757-797.

Hillman, A. and E. Katz (1984) "Risk Averse Rent-Seekers and the Social Cost of Monopoly Power," Economic Journal, 94: 104 -110.

___ and D. Samet (1987) "Rent-Seeking with Small Numbers," Public Choice.

Humana, C. -- originator and compiler -- (1986) World Human Rights Guide, The Economist, London.

Jaeger, W. and C. Humphreys (1988) "The Effect of Policy Reforms on Agricultural Incentives in Sub-Saharan Africa," American Journal of Agricultural Economics, 70(5): 1036-43.

Jaeger, W. (1989) "Policy and Growth in AfricanAgriculture: An Empirical Investigation," draft for comment.

Johnson, H. (1971) The Two-Sector Model of General Equilibium, London: George Allen & Unwin Ltd.

Johnston, J. (1972) Econometric Methods, New York: McGraw-Hill Book Company.

Jorgenson, D. and F. Griliches, (1963) "The Explanation of Productivity Change," Review of Economic Studies, December.

Jung, W. (1986) "Financial Development and Economic Growth: International Evidence," Economic Development and Cultural Change, (Jan.) 34:2: 333-346.

Kaempfer, W. and T. Willett (1989) "Combining Rent-Seeking and Public Choice Theory in the Analysis of Tariffs versus Quotas," Public Choice, 63: 79-86.

Kaldor, N. (1961) "Economic Growth and Capital Accumulation," in F. Lutz and D. Hauge, eds., The Theory of Capital, Macmillan: London

Katz, E. and Rosenberg (1989) "Rent-Seeking for Budgetary Allocation: Preliminary Results for 20 Countries," Public Choice, 60: 133-144.

Kendrick, J. and R. Sato (1963) "Factor Prices, Productivity, and Growth," American Economic Review, December.

Kmenta, Jan (1986) Elements of Econometrics, New York: Macmillan Publishing Co.

Knight, J. and R. Sabot (1988) "Lewis Through a Looking Glass: Public Sector Employment, Rent-Seeking and Economic Growth," Williams College, Center for Development Economics, Research Memorandum Series (U.S.) No. RM-108: 1 [49], January.

Kohli, A. (1986) "Democracy and Development," in Lewis, J. and V. Kallab eds. Development Strategies Reconsidered, Overseas Development Council.

Kormendi, R. and P. Meguire (1985) "Macroeconomic Determinants of Growth: Cross-Country Evidence," Journal of Monetary Economics, 16: 141-163.

Koutsoyiannis, A. (1979) Modern Microeconomics, second edition, New York: St. Martin's Press.

Kravis, I. (1970) "Trade as a Handmaiden of Growth: Similarities between the Nineteenth and Twentieth Centuries," American Economic Review, Dec.: 850-870

Krueger, A. (1974) "The Political Economy of the Rent-Seeking Society," American Economic Review June: 291-303.

Kuznets, S. (1952) "Comment" on Abramovitz, M. "Economics of Growth," in B. Haley ed. A Survey of Contemporary Economics: Vol. II, published for the American Economics Association by Richard D. Irwin, Inc.

Kuznets, S. (1966) Modern Economic Growth: Rate, Structure, and Spread, Yale University Press.

Laband, D. and J. Sophocleus (1988) "Social Cost of Rent-Seeking: First Estimates," Public Choice, 58: 269-275, September.

Landau, D. (1986) "Government and Economic Growth in the Less Developed Countries: An Empirical Study for 1960-80," Economic Development and Cultural Change 35, October: 35-76.

___ (1983) "Government Expenditure and Economic Growth: A Cross Country Study," Southern Economic Journal vol. 49, January: 783-93.

Landes, W. and R. Posner (1975) "The Independent Judiciary in an Interest-Group Perspective," Journal of Law and Economics, 18: 875-901

Levy, D. (1989) "Equilibrium Employment of Inputs by a Rent-Seeking Firm," Public Choice, 60: 177-184.

Lewis, J. and V. Kallab (1986) eds Development Strategies Reconsidered, Overseas Development Council, Washington, D.C.

Lewis, W. A. (1954) "Economic Development with Unlimited Supplies of Labor," The Manchester School.

___ (1978) The Theory of Economic Growth, twelfth impression, (original 1955).

Lindauer, D. (1988) The Size and Growth of Government Spending, World Bank Staff Working Paper Series No. 44.

Lucas, R. (1987) "On the Mechanics of Economic Development," Journal of Monetary Economics, 22: 43-70.

Mahmudul, A. (1998) "Quota-Induced Rent Seeking, Terms of Trade and National Welfare: A Paradox," Journal of Development Economics 28: 389-395.

Marsden, K. (1983) Links between Taxes and Economic Growth: Some Empirical Evidence World Bank Staff Working Paper No. 605.

Mbaku, J. and C. Paul (1989) "Political Instability in Africa: A Rent-Seeking Approach," Public Choice, 63: 63-72.

McCallum, B.T., (1970) "Artificial Orthogonalization in Regression Analysis," Review of Economics and Statistics (February) Vol. 52: 1, pp. 110-113.

Meade, J. (1961) A Neo-Classical Theory of Economic Growth, Allen and Unwin: London.

Meier, G. ed. (1983) Pricing Policy for Development, publisher for the Economic Development Institute of the World Bank, Johns Hopkins University Press.

___ and D. Seers, eds. (1984) Pioneers in Economic Development World Bank and Oxford University Press.

Mellor, J. (1986) "Agriculture on the Road to Industrialization," chapter in Lewis, J. and V.Kallab eds. Development Strategies Reconsidered, Overseas Development Council.

Michaels, R. (1988) "The Design of Rent-seeking Competitions," Public Choice, 56: 17-29.

Millner, E. and M. Pratt (1989) "An Experimental Investigation of Efficient Rent-Seeking," Public Choice, 62: 139-151.

Morrison, D., R. Mitchell, J. Paden, and H. Stevenson (1972) Black Africa: A Comparative Handbook, The Free Press, New York.

Morrison, D., R. Mitchell, and J. Paden (1989) Black Africa: A Comparative Handbook, A Washington Institute Book, Paragon Books.

Mueller, D. (1983) The Political Economy of Growth, New Haven, Conn.: Yale University Press.

___ (1987) "The Growth of Government: A Public Choice Perspective," IMF Staff Papers, 34, 1 March: 254-331.

Murphy, K., A. Schleifer, and R. Vishny (1990) "The Allocation of Talent: Implications for Growth," presented at the Conference on Economic Growth on April 12-14, at Vail, Colorada, sponsored by the National Bureau of Economic Research.

Myrdal, G. (1957) Economic Theory and Underdeveloped Regions, G. Duckworth: London.

Mwangi, K. and W. Shughart II (1989) "Political Successions and the Growth of Government," Public Choice, 62: 173-179.

Ndulu, B. (1986) "Governance and Economic Management," in R. Berg and J. Whitaker eds. Strategies for African Development, Overseas Development Council.

Niskanen, W. (1968) "The Peculiar Economics of Bureaucracy," American Economic Review, 58 (May): 293-305.

___ (1975) "Bureaucrats and Politicians," Journal of Law and Economics, 18 (December): 617-643. North, D. (1978) "A Framework for Analyzing the State in Economic History," Explorations in Economic History 16: 249-259.

Olson, Mancur (1983) "The Political Economy of Comparative Growth Rates," in D. Mueller ed. The Political Economy of Growth.

___ (undated) "Notes to be used in preparing a paper on ANARCHY, AUTOCRACY, AND IDEAL REDISTRIBUTIVE DEMOCRACY," permission to cite granted by the author on 12/15/89.

Orr, D. (1980) "Rent-Seeking in an Aging Population," in Buchanan, J., R. Tollison, and G. Tullock eds. Toward a Theory... op. cit.

Paden, J. and E. Soja eds. (1970) The African Experience, Volume I: Essays, Northwestern University Press, Evanston.

Pasour, Jr., E. (1987) "Rent-Seeking: Some Conceptual Problems and Implications," The Review of Austrian Economics, 1: 123-143.

___ (1989) "Nonconventional Costs of Rent-Seeking: X-inefficiency in the Political Process," Public Choice, 63: 87-91.

Peltzman, S. (1976) "Toward a More General Theory of Regulation," Journal of Law and Economics, 2: 211-240.

Phelps, E. (1961) "The Golden Rule of Accumulation: A Fable for Growth Men," American Economic Review, September.

___ (1962) "The New View of Investment: A Neoclassical Analysis," Quarterly Journal of Economics, November.

___ (1966) Golden Rules of Economic Growth, New York: W. W. Norton.

___ ed. (1969) The Goal of Economics Growth, New York: Norton.

Pincus, J. (1975) "Pressure Groups and the Pattern of Tariffs,"Journal of Political Economy, 83: 757-778.

Posner, R. (1975) "The Social Cost of Monopoly and Regulation," Journal of Political Economy, 83 (August): 807-827.

Prebisch, R. [Secretary General] (1950) The Economic Development of Latin America and Its Principal Problems, from the United Nations Economic Commission for Latin America (New York: United Nations).

___ (1963) "Development Problems of the Peripheral Countries and the Terms of Trade," from Toward a Dynamic Development Policy for Latin America, United Nations.

Ram, R. (1985) "Exports and Economic Growth: Some Additional Evidence," Economic Development and Cultural Change, 12: 59-74.

___ (1986) "Causality between Income and Government Expenditure: A Broad International Perspective," Public Finance no. 3:393-414.

___ (1987) "Wagner's Hypothesis in Time-Series and Cross-Section Perspectives: Evidence from 'Real' Data for 115 Countries," Reveiw of Economics and Statistics, (May) 29: 194-204.

Rowley, C. and R. Tollison (1986) "Rent-Seeking and Trade Protection," Aussenwirtschaft, (Switzerland) 41: 303-28, September.

Reid, Jr. J. (1970) "On Navigating the Navigation Acts with Peter D. McClelland: Comment," American Economic Review, 60: 949-954

___ (1977) "Understanding Political Events in the New Economic History," Journal of Economic History, Vol. 37 No. 2: 302-328.

___ (1986) "The Lessons of History for Economic Development: Mercantilism and Prosperity," Dept. of Economics, George Mason University (mimeo) April 30.

___ and M. Kurth (1989) "Public Employees in Political Firms: Part A. The Patronage Era," Public Choice, 59: 253-262.

Ricardo, David The Principles of Political Economy and Taxation, reprinted by Dent and Son, London, 1937.

Romer, P. (1986) "Increasing Returns and Long-Run Growth," Journal of Political Economy, 94: 1002-1037.

___ (1989) What Determines the Rate of Growth and Technological Change? World Bank, Working Paper Series No. 279.

Ross, V. (1984) "Rent-Seeking in LDC Import Regimes: the Case of Kenya," Graduate Institute of International Studies, Discussion Papers in International Economics, (Switzerland) 8408: 1-36, December. {copy missing, send for it}

Rubinson, R. (1977) "Dependence, Government Revenue, and Economic Growth, 1955-1970," Studies in Comparative International Development, 12: 3-28.

Sandbrook, R. (1982) The Politics of Basic Needs: Urban Aspects of Assaulting Poverty, London: Heinemann.

__ with J. Barker (1985) The Politics of Africa's Economic Stagnation, London: Cambridge University Press.

Schap, D. (1985) "X-inefficiency in a Rent-Seeking Society: a Graphical Analysis," Quarterly Review of Economics and Business, 25: 19-27, Spring.

Scholing, E. and V. Timmermann, (1988) "Why LDC Growth Rates Differ: Measuring 'Unmeasurable Influences,'"World Development 16, no. 11: 1271-1294.

Schultz, T. W. (1961) "Investment in Human Capital," American Economic Review March: 1-17.

Shrivastava, O.S. (1974) Theories and Models of Economic Development, Progress Publishers, Bhopal, India.

Silver, (1974) "Political Revolution and Repression: An Economic Approach," Public Choice, 17 (Spring): 63-70.

Smith, Adam (1776) The Wealth of Nations reprinted by Random House, New Yrok in 1937.

Solow, R. (1956) "A Contribution to the Theory of Economic Growth," Quarterly Journal of Economics, 70, February: 65-94.

__ (1957) "Technological Change and the Aggregate Production Function," Review of Economics and Statistics August.

__ (1961) "Note on Uzawa's Two Sector Model of Economic Growth," Review of Economic Studies, Vol. 29: October.

__ (1970) Growth Theory: An Exposition, Oxford University Press: New York.

Soltan, K. (1988) "Democracy, Dictatorship and Decision Costs," Public Choice, 57: 155-173.

Summers, R. and A. Heston, (1988) "A New Set of International Comparisons of Real Product and Price Levels," Review of Income and Wealth vol. 34, March.

Todaro, M. (1977) Economic Development in the Third World, Longman Inc. New York.

Tollison, R. (1982) "Rent-Seeking: A Survey," Kyklos, 35: 575-603.

Tullock, G. (1980) "Efficient Rent Seeking," in Toward a Theory of the Rent-Seeking Society, ed. J. Buchanan, R. Tollison, and G. Tullock, pp. 3-15, College Station: Texas A&M University Press.

__ (1984) "The Backward Society: Static Inefficiency, Rent-Seeking, and the Rule of Law," in The Theory of Public Choice-II.

__ (1988a) "The Costs of Rent-Seeking: A Metaphysical Problem," Public Choice, 57: 15-24.

__ (1988b) "Future Directions for Rent-Seeking Research," in C. Rowley, R. Tollison and G. Tullock (Eds.) The Political Economy of Rent-Seeking, Ch. 31. Boston, MA: Kluwer Academic Publishers.

Uzawa, H. (1961) "On a Two-sector Model of Economic Growth:I," Review of Economic Studies, Vol. 29: October.

__ (1963) "On a Two-sector Model of Economic Growth: II," Review of Economic Studies, Vol. 30: June.

Vedder, R. and L. Gallaway (1986) "Rent-Seeking, Distributional Coalitions, Taxes, Relative Prices and Economic Growth," Public Choice, 51: 93-100.

Vinod, H., (1978) "A Survey of Ridge Regression and Related Techniques for Improvements over Ordinary Least Squares," Review of Economics and Statistics, (February) Vol. 60: 1, pp. 121-131.

Wagner, A. (1890) Finanzwissenschaft, Leipzig.

Wagner, R. and W. Weber (1975) "Competition, Monopoly, and the Organization of Government in Metropolitan Areas," Journal of Law and Economics, 18: 661-684.

Wilson, J. Q. (1961) "The Economy of Patronage," Journal of Political Economy, 69: 369-380.

Wood, A. (1986) Growth and Structural Change in Large Low-Income Countries, World Bank Staff Working Paper No. 763, A Background Paper for China: Long-Term Development Issues and Options The World Bank.

World Bank (1981) Accelerated Development in Sub-Saharan Africa.

__ (1987) World Development Report 1987.

__ (1989a) World Development Report 1989.

__ (1989b) Recent Trends in Developing Countries.

__ and the United Nations Development Programme (1989a) African Economic and Financial Data.

__ and __ (1989b) Africa's Adjustment and Growth in the 1980s.

Young, C. (1987) The Politics of Cultural Pluralism, Madison, Wisconsin: The University of Wisconsin Press.

Yusuf, S. and R. Kyle Peters (1985) Capital Accumulation and Economic Growth: The Korean Paradigm, World Bank Staff Working Paper Series No. 712.

Index

181